Toward Paperless
Information Systems

Toward Paperless Information Systems

F. W. LANCASTER

Graduate School of Library Science
University of Illinois at Urbana–Champaign
Urbana, Illinois

ACADEMIC PRESS   New York   San Francisco   London   1978

A Subsidiary of Harcourt Brace Jovanovich, Publishers

ACADEMIC PRESS, INC.
111 Fifth Avenue, New York, New York 10003

United Kingdom Edition published by
ACADEMIC PRESS, INC. (LONDON) LTD.
24/28 Oval Road, London NW1 7DX

Library of Congress Cataloging in Publication Data

Lancaster, Frederick Wilfrid, Date
    Toward paperless information systems.

    (Library and information science)
    Bibliography: p.
    1. Information storage and retrieval systems.
2. Information science.   3. Communication of
technical information.   4. Communication in
science.   I. Title.   II. Series.
Z699.L353   029.7   78–51237
ISBN 0–12–436050–5

PRINTED IN THE UNITED STATES OF AMERICA

81 82   9 8 7 6 5 4 3

To my family

"We are not computerizing the old system of knowledge; we are computerizing a very new one in which the ground rules are different and in which the very act of computerization gives us facilities that we have not had before. Thus, we do not use the computer to do the jobs we wanted to do before; we use it to do the new job which arises."

Price, 1974, p. 36

"Perhaps the most important event of the next decade will be the recognition of the true value of information—the right information, reliable and relevant to our needs, available in a useful form to all those who need it."

Organisation for Economic Cooperation and Development, 1971, p. 17

"Political power and individual power in the computerized society will depend upon information."

Martin and Norman, 1970, p. 403

"We must recognize that computers, when properly interconnected, represent the greatest form of communications tool ever invented, with endless ramifications."

Thompson, 1976, p. 111

Contents

Preface

I first became interested in the possibilities of paperless information systems in 1972, when I discovered that the defense–intelligence community in the United States was already moving rather rapidly toward fully electronic systems. At that time I was able to see both the need for and the feasibility of paperless systems for the dissemination, storage, and retrieval of intelligence information. Subsequently I have come to believe that paperless systems have much wider applicability and that, within the context of scientific and technical communication, they are not only feasible but inevitable. In this book I try to summarize the achievements of the intelligence community in the implementation of paperless systems, to point to the need for such systems in the scientific and technical community, and to present a scenario of what a system of this type might look like.

I expect the book to be somewhat controversial. I know that not all readers will be able to accept the inevitability, the desirability, or even the feasibility of a world in which much of the professional communication is electronic. Five years ago I would not have been willing to accept these things myself. More recently, however, I have seen increasing evidence that we are indeed moving to a largely paperless environment and I have come to regard this as a natural evolutionary process in professional communication.

The paperless communication environment has profound implications for many individuals and institutions, including writers, publishers, libraries, information centers, and consumers of information. This book is presented in the hope that it will provoke these individuals and institutions to further study of the technological, intellectual, and social feasibility of the transition from a world of print on paper to a world of information transfer in electronic form. If I succeed in the role of provocateur, I will be satisfied.

Acknowledgments

My special thanks are due to the Central Intelligence Agency for permission to use the material presented in Chapter 3, and to King Research, Inc., Rockville, Maryland, and QEI Inc., Bedford, Massachusetts, for permission to use material I prepared for these companies in the fulfillment of various contracts with the National Science Foundation. Several publishers and authors whose illustrations and quotations I have used are also acknowledged throughout the text.

1

Introduction

Since the invention of printing from movable type in the middle of the fifteenth century, and more especially since the development of the scientific periodical some 200 years later, formal channels of professional communication have been very heavily based on printed documents. We tend to take this medium completely for granted. But can we necessarily assume that print on paper will always be the major vehicle for formal communication in science and other professional fields? Will paper be as important in the information systems of the year 2000 as it is today? Almost certainly not.

The National Science Foundation (1975) has suggested the need for a replacement for paper in the following terms: "The limits of what can be communicated by printing, mailing, storing, and retrieving pieces of paper may be at hand. Certainly, for any real improvement in the accessibility and usefulness of information an alternative must be found [p. 1]." The solution they suggest is an electronic alternative to paper-based systems: "One possibility is to capture new information from its originators in computer-sensible form and store it in central facilities for presentation at terminals wherever and whenever it would be useful [p. 1]." Something resembling an electronic (i.e., paperless) information system has been predicted by various writers for some time.

In 1945 Bush wrote a much-cited article in which he proposed a desk-top personal documentation system, known as Memex. Memex was described as a "mechanized private file and library." By means of microfilm scientists could build up large personal collections of various documents in compact form. They could add materials freely, including correspondence and personal notes, index all items in any way useful for future retrieval, consult this library "with exceeding speed and flexibility" through the use of a keyboard, and build into it "associative trails" resulting from heuristic searching. Licklider (1965), discussing "libraries of the future," conceptualized a somewhat similar but more advanced system, known as Symbiont. Symbiont was visualized as a system based on the use of on-line computer facilities. Through individual on-line terminals users could search document files, browse through documents in machine-readable form, extract or highlight passages of text by the use of the light pen, annotate documents, compose graphs from tabulated data, and perform various other manipulations of text or numerical data.

Bagdikian (1971) suggested that the production of major newspapers in digital form may lead to alternative methods of news distribution, including the possibility of transmitting a newspaper, or selected portions of it, to a customer's television set. Experimental systems for the delivery of news to the home electronically now exist. They include the Ceefax system of the British Broadcasting Corporation and the Reuters News View. Future prospects for electronic replacements for the newspaper are touched upon by Moghdam (1978).

Kemeny (1972) too discussed the possibility of a personalized, computer-based newspaper, one completely up to date and capable of bringing to a particular user the news items that *he* wants to see. Kemeny also referred to a "national automated reference library" into which scientific papers, instead of being published in conventional printed journals, would be "inserted directly ... and be immediately available to anyone who cared to retrieve them [p. 88]."

Landau (1972) described a "library in a desk." The executive type of desk (see Figure 1) incorporates two modules, one a computer terminal and the other a microfilm reader. The terminal is potentially connectable to any on-line retrieval system through a normal telephone circuit. After the user identifies relevant document references, by searching the remote machine-readable files accessible through his[1] terminal, he can turn to the microform store (in the desk drawers) and mount the selected

[1] The masculine pronoun is used throughout this book in contexts where use of a singular pronoun cannot be reasonably avoided. There is no neuter personal pronoun in English, and the use of "he" or "his" is not intended to imply that any positions so denoted are in the sole domain of men.

Figure 1. The "Library in a Desk." (Reproduced by permission of Robert Landau.)

microform (microfiche or microfilm cartridge) in the viewer-selector for rapid viewing of the desired documents. Various levels of sophistication are possible in the equipment. The least elaborate model would have a typewriter terminal and a manual microform viewer. A more elaborate model would incorporate a CRT display and a microform viewer having automatic image selection and printing capabilities. In the most elaborate configuration of this type, the user might view document images transmitted to his station from a remote microform store by means of closed-circuit television or some other transmission device.

These various conceptualizations have much in common. They all represent information storage, transmission, and retrieval systems that are largely paperless—systems in which paper is replaced by microform, by documents in digital form, by television images, or by a combination of these. Moreover, the systems of Bush, Licklider, and Landau assume that the user will have, literally at his fingertips, access to a large personal library and/or to a wide range of external bibliographic resources.

If any group has need for a paperless information system, and if any is in the best position to implement such a system, it is the intelligence community. The need exists because the volume of documents routinely processed by this community amounts to several thousand each day, a considerably greater number than those processed by the largest science information systems, and because these documents need to be disseminated, evaluated, and acted upon very rapidly. The opportunity exists because a substantial proportion of the documents handled by this community is transmitted by wire communication systems and thus can be captured, at point of arrival, in digital (machine-readable) form.

Since 1973, or thereabouts, work has proceeded at the Central Intelligence Agency toward a largely paperless information handling system, a system which will disseminate intelligence messages in digital form to on-line viewing stations and will permit the recipient to discard messages, store messages, index them, extract from them, comment on them, or bring them to the attention of other users, all these activities taking place at an on-line terminal and all involving digital text. In addition, the on-line terminal will give the user access to a wide range of other data bases, within the Agency or from outside sources, some of these being indexed representations of documents and others being files of complete text in digital form. The use of microforms also plays an important part in the system. This system has been implemented on a small scale, has been evaluated, and has been shown to be feasible. Work is now proceeding toward the design of an Agency-wide system, based on the prototype, which will support the work of about 2000 intelligence analysts through the use of several hundred on-line terminals. This system represents a significant step toward the implementation of paperless systems on the much broader scale suggested later in this book.

This book briefly summarizes achievements in the application of computers to information retrieval since 1963, reviews the status of the application of paperless systems within the intelligence community, discusses the feasibility of paperless systems for scientific and technical communication, presents a scenario for a possible system of the year 2000, and concludes with the identification of various problems that need to be solved before the paperless systems of the future can be fully realized.

2

The Application of Computers
to the Storage, Retrieval, and
Dissemination of Information

This chapter gives a broad overview of developments that have taken place in computer retrieval, and related activities, since 1963. It presents some necessary background for the matters discussed in later chapters, and defines some terms, but it contains nothing that is likely to be new to those already active in the field of information processing. It may therefore be omitted by readers with extensive experience in this field.

The term *information retrieval*, as it is commonly used, refers to the activities involved in searching a body of literature in order to find items (i.e., documents of one kind or another) that deal with a particular subject area. An *information retrieval system*, then, is any tool or device that organizes a body of literature in such a way that it can be searched conveniently. Most information retrieval systems do not store and search documents themselves. Rather, they store some representation or surrogate of each document: a bibliographic citation (with perhaps an abstract) together with one or more indicators of subject content. These indicators may be numeric or alphanumeric codes from a classification scheme, subject headings, keywords, or, more commonly in modern information systems, *descriptors* selected from a thesaurus.

If we accept the preceding definitions, it is clear that information retrieval systems have existed for a very long time, at least as long as we

5

have had printed indexes or the catalogs of libraries in book or card form. The term *information retrieval* itself, however, is of relatively new vintage, having apparently been coined by Calvin Mooers in 1950 or thereabouts.

Off-Line Processing

The first application of computers to information retrieval occurred in the 1950s, although it was not until the following decade that these devices came into their own in this field. At that time a number of major systems were developed in the United States, notably by the Defense Documentation Center (then known as the Armed Services Technical Information Agency), the National Aeronautics and Space Administration, and the National Library of Medicine. The system developed by the National Library of Medicine—the Medical Literature Analysis and Retrieval System (MEDLARS)—was the largest of these, both in terms of the size of its files (growing at the rate of over 200,000 items a year) and in terms of the population served; MEDLARS was implemented in 1964. The computer-based systems for information retrieval developed in the 1960s were similar in many respects. They were operated in an off-line, batch processing mode, and the computer itself served merely as a device for matching the characteristics of documents (e.g., the index terms assigned to them) against the characteristics of requests for information. The matching itself was achieved by the serial searching of magnetic tape.

All the intellectual processing in such systems is conducted by humans and it is, of course, the intellectual processing and not the machine processing that controls the performance of the system. By "intellectual processing" we mean: (a) the activities involved in the conceptual analysis of documents and the translation of these conceptual analyses into the terms of some limited or *controlled* vocabulary (e.g., a thesaurus of descriptors), a process generally referred to as *subject indexing;* (b) the transformation of requests for information into formal searching strategies consisting of descriptors, or other index terms, in specified logical relationships (the relationships of Boolean algebra); (c) the construction and maintenance of the controlled vocabulary of the system; and (d) the interaction between the information specialists in the system and the community of users, whereby these users (*requesters*) make their needs known to the system.

The computer plays a comparatively minor role in such systems since, apart from its possible application to error detection in indexing and to various housekeeping functions, it is used only in the searching component of the complete system, and there only to effect a match between document representation and request representation. Moreover, the computer has virtually no influence on the effectiveness of the information retrieval system. The effectiveness of the system, its ability to retrieve documents relevant to particular information needs, is governed by the intellectual factors rather than by machine processing factors. Nevertheless, the computer has had a very beneficial effect on the cost-effectiveness of information retrieval systems and upon their overall efficiency (e.g., in terms of search time). In fact, computer-based systems offered very significant advantages over earlier retrieval systems, including the ability to handle extremely large files, conduct many searches at the same time (through *batch processing*), provide multiple access points to documents conveniently and economically, conduct comprehensive and exhaustive searches, produce printed lists of retrieved citations or even high-quality published indexes (through photocomposition), produce microfilm output (computer-output micro-film), generate system management information, and—perhaps most important of all—create machine-readable files that can easily be shipped to other users, thus making them widely accessible through net-working or other cooperative activities or through licensing and leasing agreements.

In terms of information transfer, the single most important develop-ment that has occurred since 1960 has been the emergence of the machine-readable bibliographic data base. Many of the major informa-tion processing systems developed in this period were designed primarily as publication systems, particularly systems to produce printed indexes or abstracts journals. MEDLARS was the pioneering system in this respect, being designed primarily to produce a major printed index (*Index Medicus*) by the use of a computer. In fact, in developing MEDLARS, the National Library of Medicine supported the design and implementation of the first device used in a large production environment for photocom-position under computer control. To photocompose a printed index it is first necessary to put the indexing records into machine-readable form. Once this is done, and the index produced, say on a monthly basis, the publisher has available (as essentially a by-product of the publication process) a machine-readable data base that can be used for other pur-poses, including the generation of other publications and the provision of a machine literature searching capability.

The National Library of Medicine pointed the way and many other organizations followed. Printed indexes and abstracts journals are now produced routinely by photocomposition procedures under computer control and many important machine-readable bibliographic data bases now exist as a result, including those of the Chemical Abstracts Service, Biological Abstracts, the Engineering Index, the Science Citation Index, Psychological Abstracts, and Excerpta Medica. By a conservative estimate, over 500 machine-readable data bases were being used in the provision of information services in 1978. These files range in scope from those dealing with entire scientific disciplines, like chemistry or medicine, to some in highly specialized subject areas, such as epilepsy, tall buildings, and interatomic potentials. Not only have these data bases been created, but the producers have also been extremely active in making them available to other users through leasing, licensing, or other arrangements.

A machine-readable data base can be used in a number of different ways in the provision of information service. It can be used to generate printed indexes, to conduct retrospective searches, or to provide a selective dissemination of information (SDI) service. A retrospective search, as its name implies, is a search through a body of past literature in order to find items on some specific or general topic. (A retrospective search, which is conducted only when a demand is made by a particular individual, is sometimes referred to as a *demand search*.) An SDI service, however, is concerned only with recently published literature. It is a type of current awareness or alerting service. In SDI, the current subject interests of users are converted into searching strategies, usually referred to as *user interest profiles*. These profiles are stored in machine-readable form. When new additions are made to a data base, say on a monthly basis, these additions are matched by computer against the stored interest profiles. Records that match the interests of particular individuals are printed out and mailed to them, thus enabling them to keep up to date on a regular basis in their fields of specialization.

An SDI service may be regarded as the obverse of a retrospective searching service. In the latter, document representations are stored and matched, on demand, with specific requests for information. In the former, requests for information ("standing requests") are stored and matched against incoming document representations. The use of computers in SDI has been extremely successful and has created a revolution in the provision of information service. When operating in a batch processing mode, SDI is much more attractive economically than retrospective searching because the system is dealing at any one time with relatively small document files (i.e., the latest input only). Retrospective searching, on the other hand, may involve the searching of extremely large data bases (in excess of a million records) spanning several years, and very much more computer processing is involved. SDI, then, is relatively inexpensive when compared with the retrospective searching of very large data bases, at least when the sequential searching of magnetic tapes is involved.

On-Line Processing

The term *off-line*, as applied to an information system, refers to the fact that the searcher is not in direct communication with the data base or with the computer by which this data base is manipulated. That is, the user prepares a searching strategy away from the data base and without being able to interact with it. This searching strategy is put into machine-readable form, batched with others, and "run" when computer time becomes available. Under the best of conditions the "turnaround time" is likely to be overnight and very frequently it may involve a delay of some days. It is not until he receives a printout of the search results that the user can determine whether or not his search has been successful. If it is judged unsuccessful, he must go through the whole process a second time, modifying his strategy on the basis of this delayed feedback from the system.

It is clear that off-line systems for retrospective searching (but not necessarily for SDI) have significant disadvantages. The response time may be unsatisfactory for any but the user involved in a relatively long-term project; the system provides no capability for browsing; in constructing his strategy the searcher is operating "blind" without being able to develop the strategy in an interactive, heuristic manner; and, finally, the real system user (i.e., the person with the information need) is unable to conduct his own search but must delegate this responsibility to an information specialist who knows how to interrogate the system.

On-line information retrieval systems have none of these disadvantages. In an on-line system the users are in direct communication with the computer and with the data base they wish to interrogate. They communicate by means of a terminal, which may be a simple typewriter terminal or some type of video display (e.g., cathode ray tube or plasma panel) with associated keyboard, connected to the computer by means of communication lines. Because these communication lines can be regular telephone lines, the terminal can be far removed physically (e.g., several thousand miles) from the computer itself.

Through time-sharing, an on-line system can support multiple simultaneous users, giving each of these (most of the time) the illusion that he is the sole user of the system. Response in an on-line system is immediate rather than delayed. That is, an on-line system can respond very rapidly to a user command, typically in 5 seconds or less. On-line systems can thus be used for searches in which users need information right away (e.g., a physician needing information to deal with an immediate clinical problem), whereas off-line systems are really of value only to users to whom response time is relatively unimportant. Moreover, the on-line searcher can interact directly with the data base, developing his strategy as he goes along on a trial-and-error basis (i.e., heuristically). Searching errors are less serious in an on-line system than they are in an off-line system because they can be identified and corrected quite rapidly. Finally, because terminals can be made widely available, and because languages of interrogation can be kept relatively simple, on-line systems can be used in a nondelegated mode. That is, the scientist, intelligence analyst, or other professional who has need of information can conduct his own search at the terminal if he so desires. This is a significant advantage: One of the major problems of a delegated search system is that the user may not be able to describe clearly, to an information specialist, what it is he is looking for, or the information specialist may misinterpret the request of the user.

Some experiments with on-line information retrieval were made in the early 1960s, notably at the Massachusetts Institute of Technology, and a number of important systems were developed in the late 1960s, including Lockheed's DIALOG and the implementation of this system by the National Aeronautics and Space Administration (NASA) as RECON (Remote Console). On-line systems for information retrieval have really come into their own in the 1970s, however, and in the last 5 years we have seen a fairly widespread conversion of systems from off-line to on-line processing. A notable example was the conversion of MEDLARS to MEDLARS On-Line (MEDLINE), a system supporting several hundred terminals in the United States and elsewhere. Conversion of MEDLARS to MEDLINE increased the volume of use of this data base in the United States from about 20,000 searches a year to about 20,000 searches a month. Many of these developments have been discussed in detail in an earlier book by Lancaster and Fayen (1973).

The Growth of Information Services Based on Machine-Readable Files

As indicated earlier, the emergence of the machine-readable data base has caused a major revolution in the provision of information service. If we accept the MEDLARS data base as being the first to be made widely available, beginning in 1965, there has been in one decade a growth of machine-readable files, of possible utility in the provision of information service, from one to somewhere in excess of 500. The National Library of Medicine (NLM) made its MEDLARS data base widely available through cooperative arrangements with other institutions, mostly medical libraries. Beginning with the University of Colorado Medical Center in 1965, NLM established a network of MEDLARS centers throughout the United States, each center being responsible for service to a designated geographic region. Very soon this network was extended beyond the United States, with MEDLARS centers being established in Sweden, England, France, Germany, Switzerland, Canada, Australia, Japan, and elsewhere. The foreign centers, and some of the centers in the United States, had their own computer facilities. The data base was shipped to these centers in tape form and updated monthly. The individual center would use the tapes for retrospective searching and, in some cases, the provision of SDI service. The centers without computer facilities acted only as search centers. Search strategies were prepared there by trained analysts, but the searches themselves were run on the computer facilities of NLM or some other MEDLARS center.

As more and more of the wholesalers of information (i.e., the producers of the major indexing and abstracting services) have implemented photocomposition procedures, more and more data bases have become available. Many of these data bases can be leased by individual organizations in order to provide information services within the organization itself. Thus, a large chemical company might lease a data base from the Chemical Abstracts Service, a large engineering concern from Engineering Index, Inc., and so on. Once acquired, the data base can be used to provide SDI and retrospective search services for the research and development staff of the organization itself.

Unfortunately, it is relatively expensive to lease the larger data bases and only very large organizations are likely to be able to afford this luxury, or to have a volume of in-house demand sufficient to justify the investment. This fact led to the development, in the 1960s, of a completely new kind of information center, the *scientific information dissemination center* (SIDC). An SIDC is a center, usually located in a university, that enters into licensing arrangements with several data base producers. A licensing arrangement provides the center with the data base and with authorization to provide services, on a fee basis, to any who wish to use them. SDI service is emphasized by these centers (examples exist at the University of Georgia, the Illinois Institute of Technology, the University of California at Los Angeles, Nottingham University in England, and Karolinska Institutet in Stockholm), but retrospective searches are also conducted on demand. The costs of information service are very volume-dependent, and these centers are able to charge at a reasonable rate by generating a high level of demand from a wide audience of institutional and individual users. Moreover, these centers provide a convenient single source through which service can be obtained from a number of different data bases. Thus, a research group can have its interest profile matched on a regular basis against two or more files.

The advent of on-line retrieval capabilities vastly increased the accessibility of machine-readable files. One of the pioneers of on-line information service was NASA, which made its important data base on the space and related sciences available in the late 1960s through its RECON (Remote Console) system, an adaptation of Lockheed's DIALOG. Although RECON is an important system, it had limited impact on the library and .information world in general because its use was largely restricted to NASA facilities and NASA contractors in the United States. The system was later used, however, by other organizations for further information services, in Europe as well as in America. A more important development, in terms of impact, was MEDLINE, the on-line version of MEDLARS, which was implemented by the National Library of Medicine in 1971. MEDLINE, which is based on ORBIT, a commercially available software system developed by the System Development Corporation, is particularly important because of its accessibility. In 1978 the system is being used by several hundred medical libraries and other institutions in the United States, with other users located in Europe and elsewhere. MEDLINE was the first system to be widely integrated into library services, and many medical librarians are now using it routinely for literature searching as a logical extension of their traditional printed tools. MEDLINE gives them a searching capability much more powerful than any they have had in the past.

MEDLINE is an example of an on-line system in which the users have access to a remote data base that is physically maintained by the producer of that data base. Another important system of this type is the *New York Times* Information Bank, which provides subscribers with on-line access to a most important data base in the field of current affairs.

A later development is the emergence of the on-line retailer of information services. The on-line retailer operates in much the same way as a scientific information dissemination center. The retailer acquires data bases through licensing agreements, loads them on its own computer facilities, and sells access to these files on the basis of the resources used. Thus, the on-line retailer provides a convenient single source through which many data bases may be interrogated. Three major on-line retailers—the System Development Corporation, Lockheed Information Systems, and Bibliographic Retrieval Services—now provide access to a wide range of bibliographic services in the sciences and the social sciences.

The latest trend in this evolutionary process is the concept of a regional information center through which scientists, using their own academic or industrial libraries, are given access to a great number of resources in machine-readable form. These services can be made available at a number of different levels within a region. Some data bases can be brought into the region and operated, on-line or off-line, on computer facilities in the region itself. For other data bases, service may be purchased from an existing supplier: the data base producer, or a retailer operating in an off-line or an on-line mode. Some data bases will be accessed, from the regional center and/or from some of the larger libraries within the region, by means of on-line connections with the producer of the data base. For the less frequently used data bases it will be sufficient that the regional center should be able to obtain service, from the data base producer or some other center, when the need arises. In the long run, a regional center of this kind should be capable of guaranteeing any scientist in the region access to any data base needed for current awareness or retrospective search purposes and, because of the volume of demand in the region as a whole, should be able to keep the costs of such service reasonably low. An important element in this scheme is the role played by academic and industrial libraries in the overall provision of information services. It is to his or her own library that the individual scientist turns when the need for information arises. The staff of each library must therefore include people who know the full range of resources that are available in machine-readable form and how to obtain service from these files. The "information services librarian," a professional whose major responsibility is the exploitation of machine-readable data bases, is becoming a recognized area of specialization within the field of library science. A regional center of the general type outlined above was set up experimentally in the northeast United States. This center, known as NASIC (the Northeast Academic Science Information Center), was established by the New England Board of Higher Education with funds provided by the National Science Foundation.

Through developments such as these, the use of computer-based services is becoming increasingly commonplace in libraries and other types of information centers. Although academic and industrial libraries have been most affected, there is also some use of such services in public libraries, at least on an experimental basis.

Natural Language Searching

So far this discussion has assumed the use of data bases consisting of document representations or surrogates. The document surrogate will typically consist of a bibliographic citation and a list of index terms representing the subject matter of the document. Usually the index terms assigned to the document by an indexer will be selected from some form of controlled vocabulary, such as a thesaurus. It is also possible to operate a retrieval system without using a controlled vocabulary. For example, titles, titles plus abstracts, or even the complete text of a document collection, can be stored and searched by computer. Searches are conducted on any combinations of words occurring in the stored text. A retrieval system that operates on words occurring in titles, abstracts, or text may be referred to as a *natural language* or *free text* system. If the complete text of a collection is available for searching in digital form, the system is best termed a *full text* retrieval system.

Computers have been used in full text searching for some time, particularly in the field of law. The groundwork was laid at the Health Law Center of the University of Pittsburgh, which began, about 1960, by putting the statutes of the State of Pennsylvania into machine-readable form and went on to add further substantial bodies of legal text. The success of this operation is attested to by its later conversion to a commercial enterprise (the Aspen Systems Corporation) and by its adoption by the Department of Defense as Project LITE (Legal Information Through Electronics). More and more natural language data bases have become available as by-products of the publication of indexes and abstracts journals, and considerable experience has been accumulated in the searching of data bases of this type, particularly by the scientific information dissemination centers. Some of these data bases are searched only on words occurring in titles; others are searched on words appearing in abstracts.

Natural language searching systems are of two principal types. In the first type, the data base is stored on magnetic tape and the complete text is searched sequentially. This type of sequential search of text is most suitable for off-line, batch processing applications where response time is not critical. It is particularly appropriate for use in SDI services because only a relatively small data base needs to be processed at any one time. The serial searching of very large data bases of text, in order to handle retrospective searches, is a more expensive proposition.

The second type of natural language system is not searched sequentially. Instead, the computer is used to construct a text "concordance" which shows exactly where each word occurs (document number, line number, word number) in the data base. Searches are conducted in this concordance. That is, the lists of document numbers appearing under terms in the concordance (the complete lists of terms, with document numbers associated with each, are referred to as an *inverted file*) are compared by computer so that common numbers, representing documents in which two or more sought words are known to co-occur, can be identified. The inverted file approach is necessary in order to provide the rapid response needed in an on-line system used for retrospective searching. A number of on-line natural language systems now exist. A notable example is the Data Central System, a set of programs that have been used to provide on-line access to a number of important natural language data bases, including LEXIS, a major data base in the field of law.

The techniques of searching natural language systems differ somewhat from those used in searching controlled vocabulary systems. A technique of great importance is word fragment searching—i.e., the ability to search on parts of words (prefixes, suffixes, or infixes). Also important are word distance indicators or *metric operators*, which allow the searcher to specify how close two words must be in text before they are considered to be related. The techniques of natural language searching are discussed in more detail in an earlier book by Lancaster (1972).

Automatic Information Retrieval Systems

In the great majority of machine retrieval systems, the computer plays a comparatively minor role. It merely matches a humanly prepared searching strategy against a humanly prepared document representation. A considerable amount of research has also been done on more fully automatic systems in which the computer is used to conduct some of the intellectual tasks normally performed by humans (e.g., indexing, abstracting, the classification of terms, and the automatic construction or elaboration of searching strategies). Early work on automatic indexing and extracting was conducted by Luhn and Baxendale at IBM in the late 1950s, and many further experiments have taken place since that time. Most of the techniques for automatic indexing make use of word frequency as the basis for the machine extraction of words from text. Some significant work on the automatic grouping of words (in order to form a kind of machine-prepared thesaurus) has been conducted at Cambridge, England, by Needham (1961) and by Sparck Jones (1971). Related work has been done by several investigators in so-called *associative retrieval*. In an associative system, strengths of association are computed for each term in the data base with every other term based on the extent to which the two terms occur together in documents or in document surrogates. A search strategy may consist merely of an unstructured list of terms representing the subject matter sought. The associative system accepts this list of terms and expands the strategy by pulling in additional terms that correlate highly with all of the "starting terms." As a result, the final set of documents retrieved will contain some, hopefully relevant to the request, that have been indexed under terms other than those that appeared in the original search strategy. Some of the most interesting work on associative retrieval was conducted by Stiles (1961) and Salisbury and Stiles (1969) at the National Security Agency.

Examples of systems that are more or less automatic (in that human processing is minimized or eliminated) are BROWSER, an IBM system developed by Williams (1969), LEADER or LEADERMART, a system developed by Hillman (1973) at Lehigh University, and SMART, developed by Salton (1968) at Harvard and Cornell. The first two of these were designed for on-line implementation. Although they differ greatly in specific mode of operation, and in degree of sophistication, these systems also have much in common. They all operate on text, usually abstracts, and reduce this to a searchable surrogate. BROWSER reduces the text to words or word roots having weights that reflect the frequency with which these occur in the collection as a whole (the rarest words get highest weights). LEADER reduces text to noun phrases, and SMART has a number of processing options, the most basic being the reduction of text to weighted word roots and the automatic assignment of thesaurus group numbers to a document. All three systems will accept an inquiry made in sentence form. The more complete this free statement of information need, the better the system is likely to operate. Searching in these systems is essentially a pattern matching operation. That is, the system looks for document surrogates that best match the characteristics of the request statement and retrieves these in a ranked order, those that match more closely being the first to be printed out or displayed. Fairly complete accounts of automatic indexing procedures have been made by Stevens (1970) and Sparck Jones (1974). A more concise account is given by Lancaster (1972).

This chapter has attempted a broad overview of some of the most important developments in the application of computers to information retrieval in the period 1960–1977. This is intended to provide necessary background for the discussion of developments in the intelligence community, and for the description of the characteristics of paperless systems.

3

Implementation of
a Paperless System in
the Intelligence Community

This chapter reviews the dissemination, storage, and retrieval needs of the intelligence analyst and describes the concept of a paperless information system to support the needs of this professional. Many different approaches have been made to the handling of information throughout the intelligence community. This discussion is restricted to work that has been conducted within the last 5 years at the Central Intelligence Agency.

As the name implies, the major function of the *production analyst* is to create "finished" intelligence products. A finished intelligence product may be a briefing, a short report in a daily or weekly intelligence bulletin, or a rather complete report on a situation of current interest. These products may relate to scientific subjects, economic matters, military or defense matters, technological or industrial developments, political and sociological topics, medicine and health care, or information of a biographical nature. The coverage is comprehensive in terms of its geographic scope. An individual production analyst is likely to be a specialist in a particular geographic area and in a particular type of information relating to that region.

The analyst is involved in three major activities: acquisition of materials; analysis, interpretation, and synthesis of these materials; and

17

the generation of finished intelligence products. Some of the most important raw materials for the intelligence analyst are the literally thousands of "messages" arriving at the Central Intelligence Agency each day. These messages come from a very wide range of worldwide sources. Examples are State Department cables, cables from military sources, and reports derived from the monitoring of foreign broadcasts (the Foreign Broadcast Information Service, or FBIS). The intelligence information contained in many of these sources is largely unevaluated. This is called *raw intelligence*. For some types of analysts public sources of information (e.g., newspapers) will be of some importance. This type of information is referred to as *open source*. The majority of the information, however, is not open source. Rather, it is contained in series of documents that are "classified" in a security sense.

A large proportion of these documents (perhaps about 70%) arrive "electrically," over wire communication lines. These are referred to as *electricals*. Those that arrive in the Agency in paper form are called *hard copy*. An Agency-wide dissemination system exists to ensure that the thousands of incoming documents are directed to the offices or individuals that need to see them. Much of this activity is handled by human disseminators, who work from printed "interest profiles" compiled to represent the current intelligence interests of each "dissemination point" (individual or office) within the Agency. That is, the disseminators examine incoming messages, match the contents of the messages with the interests of the dissemination points, and assign codes to each message to indicate the dissemination points to which it is to be directed. Through great experience in this task, the disseminator will have committed much of the content of the interest profiles to memory and will only occasionally need to refer to printed tools. Each message is duplicated in as many paper copies as there are recipients indicated by the disseminator (even those arriving electrically are printed in multiple copies), and these copies reach their destinations in the Agency within hours after they first arrive. High priority messages, however, are given special treatment and disseminated more rapidly. On the average, each message goes to about 14 recipients. The total number of messages disseminated a year is close to 2 million. This means that some 28 million paper copies are created and disseminated annually. Within the last few years a system has been developed that will disseminate a significant number of the incoming electricals automatically by computer, and will suggest dissemination points for others. This machine-aided dissemination will be described later in the chapter.

Through these dissemination activities, the individual analyst is likely to have a large number of messages directed to him each day. This is his daily "mail." It is an important function of the analyst to examine his daily mail and to react to it. Some items can be immediately discarded. Others, however, will require some action from the analyst. The viewing of incoming mail may lead to the production by the analyst of finished intelligence: items to appear in daily or weekly intelligence bulletins, ad hoc memoranda, briefings, or longer-term, more complete intelligence reports. Finished intelligence is produced as a result of the analysis, evaluation, and interpretation of raw intelligence and of open-source materials. Most of the analyst's time is spent in reading, evaluating, taking notes, consulting with colleagues, and in the actual writing of reports.

Another important activity is file building. While some of the messages arriving on the analyst's desk may not be worth retention, others will be. Many messages will be kept for future reference. These messages, perhaps with the analyst's comments or annotations, will be placed in personal or office files under appropriately selected headings or codes. These personal or office files will be the most important source of information that the analyst has. He will constantly refer to his files. He will use them in writing his reports, and the information contained in newly arriving messages will be compared with information already existing in the files. The personal or office files will be the first source to which an analyst turns when the need for information arises. These paper copy files are widespread throughout the Agency. Millions of copies of documents exist in the many branches of the organization. A single, relatively small branch, with only three or four analysts, may accumulate files of several hundred thousand items. The files are space consuming and duplicative in that the same document may be filed by many different analysts. It has been estimated that about 27% of all copies disseminated are filed by someone. This means that, throughout the Agency as a whole, paper copy files are growing at the rate of several million items a year.

Other Information Sources

The analyst has many other information sources available within the Agency if he chooses to use them. The most comprehensive of these is an Agency-wide information storage and retrieval system which was operated in an off-line batch processing mode for a number of years. More recently this was converted to an on-line mode of operation. Indexed into this system are the more important raw intelligence documents coming into the Agency from all sources, as well as the finished intelligence products of the Agency and of other producers of intelligence. Each document is indexed under one or more codes representing geographic area, one or more relatively broad subject codes, and key words selected from the text of the message itself. The system comprises an extremely large and important data base of intelligence information. It is available for the use of any analyst in the Agency, and information specialists are available to translate the needs of the analyst into appropriate searching strategies. Various other Agency-wide files are also available, including important and extensive files of foreign biographic information and files on foreign industrial and other installations. For some years too the Agency has been building files of complete text, in various subject areas, to meet the needs of individual analysts or branches. These files are created from incoming electrical messages. Certain categories of messages, arriving over wire communications lines, are captured in digital form on magnetic tape. Special files of various kinds can be built in this way (e.g., all messages from a particular source or all messages in a particular subject area, selected on a profile match basis). These files are generally created for the use of particular individuals or branches.

In addition to the files available in the Agency itself, a number of outside data bases can be accessed by on-line terminals located in the headquarters building. These include widely available data bases such as MEDLINE and the *New York Times* Information Bank as well as various intelligence data bases compiled by other agencies or by the intelligence community at large. An example of this type of data base is CIRCOL (the Central Information Reference and Control System On-Line), an intelligence system operated by the Foreign Technology Division, Air Force Systems Command, Wright–Patterson Air Force Base. These online systems are available for exploitation by Agency analysts, usually by requesting that a search be conducted by an information specialist, but in some cases the analyst may visit a terminal and conduct his own search.

Evaluation Activities

In 1969 an evaluation of the Agency-wide retrieval system revealed that the system seemed to be operating quite effectively for those analysts who used it. The indexing procedures, based on a combination of area codes, subject codes, and keywords, appeared to be quite effective in meeting the information needs of the analyst users. It was discovered, however, that the system was not as widely used within the

Agency as it should have been. Many analysts apparently made no use of the system at all. There seemed to be several reasons why the system was underused. First, there was some evidence that many analysts were unaware of the system or, at least, of its true capabilities. Second, the system was not immediately at hand. That is, the analyst had to make some effort to use it. Usually he or she had to make a visit to the central reference facilities of the Agency (the Central Reference Service or CRS) to discuss the information need with the specialist who was to construct the search strategy by which the system would be interrogated. Third, although the "turnaround time" was very rapid, usually 24 hours, the system was not suitable for use in cases in which the analyst needed information immediately. Fourth, and most important, there was some evidence that many analysts felt that their own files were complete and that they did not need to go to a central source of this type. A follow-up study, conducted to test this final assumption, revealed that use of the central system could be of considerable value to most of the analysts and that, in some cases at least, it could retrieve some major value items of which the analysts were not previously aware. This study cast considerable doubt on the claim that the files of individual analysts were complete and indicated that, in some cases, analysts were preparing finished intelligence documents without exhausting the full information resources of the Agency. At the same time, the investigation indicated that there were certain categories of documents that, although regarded by individual analysts as of great importance, were not routinely and completely covered in the central system.

Machine-Aided Dissemination

A series of experiments, conducted over a period of 4 years, led to the introduction of a machine-aided dissemination system (MAD), which has the following characteristics:

1. A computer is used to capture the electricals as they are received by teletype in the Agency. At hourly intervals the collection tapes are dismounted and run through a preprocessing program which detects and corrects certain types of errors and inserts various control codes.
2. A message stream of several hundred items per day is processed by the system. Dissemination is effected by matching user interest profiles, in natural language form, against the full text of incoming messages.

3. About 50% of these messages can be disseminated completely automatically on the basis of stored user interest profiles. These are "standard items," messages occurring in well-defined series that are always to be disseminated to particular offices or individuals within the Agency. For example, a hypothetical "Worldwide Meteorological Data Report," appearing weekly, would automatically be disseminated to the same group of addresses each week. The human disseminators do not see or handle the stream of messages disseminated in this way.

4. About 75% of the remaining messages can have "tentative assignments" made by computer on the basis of stored user interest profiles. The profiles consist of text words or word fragments combined by OR, AND, and NOT operators, and they specify where in a message the word combinations must occur before the message is to be disseminated. Word proximity indicators can also be included in the profile. After machine assignment of addressee codes, the messages are displayed on CRT terminals for viewing by human disseminators. The CRT device has a split screen with the message text displayed on the top part and the dissemination symbols (trigraphs representing addressees) assigned by computer displayed at the bottom of the screen. The human disseminator checks the machine assignment and approves it, modifies it, or adds to it. In the case of a message in which the computer has been unable to make an assignment, the disseminator supplies all addressee symbols at his or her keyboard.

5. Messages are printed in multiple paper copies and a courier system carries the copies to all addressees indicated. Each customer's batch of messages has a computer-printed cover showing full customer name and address as well as the telephone number of the dissemination group. Analysts are encouraged to phone this number to provide feedback on the relevance of items disseminated to them. Interest profiles may then be modified on the basis of this feedback.

6. The interest profiles of several hundred Agency analysts are stored and manipulated by the system.

7. The same system is used for file building purposes. Messages of a particular type (by subject or by source) can be read-off onto magnetic tape for use in subsequent retrospective search activities. That is, special purpose full text files are built in areas of interest to selected offices in the Agency.

The Relationship between Personal Files and Central Files

As a result of the evaluation activities mentioned earlier, considerable thought was given to the relationships between the hard copy files maintained by individual analysts and the central machine-readable files of document surrogates (with the documents themselves available from a microform store). It seemed clear that both types of systems had certain advantages, as summarized in Table 1. The disadvantages of the personal files are equivalent to the advantages of the central system, and vice versa. The major advantages of the personal files are that they are immediately accessible to the analyst (he can use them without the need to leave his office and without having to deal with some system intermediary) and they are organized to reflect his own personal and specialized viewpoint. Moreover, the personal files contain only items that the analyst has evaluated and considers to be particularly important. For certain types of relatively simple searches, the personal files are capable of giving a rapid response.

There are, however, significant disadvantages associated with these personal paper copy files. They are extremely bulky and they are duplicative in that some documents will be filed in multiple locations within the organization. Personal or office files are not widely accessible to other analysts in the Agency. Moreover, when a particular analyst leaves, his files may not be fully comprehensible to his successor or to other analysts in his branch. The evaluation studies had also suggested that many personal files are not comprehensive and that an analyst relying entirely on his or her own collection would not be exhausting the full

TABLE 1

Personal Files versus Central Files

Advantages of the personal paper copy files	Advantages of the central computer-based retrieval system
1. Immediately accessible.	1. More comprehensive than the personal files.
2. Evaluated by the analyst.	2. Can provide multiple access points conveniently and economically.
3. Organized to represent a personal viewpoint.	3. Economical of space.
4. Fairly rapid response.	4. Accessible to all.
	5. Consistency and continuity assured.
	6. Nonduplicative (a document and its surrogate are filed only once).

information resources of the Agency. Most important of all, however, is the fact that manual files are pigeonhole systems that can provide only a very limited number of access points. In fact, the majority of items are filed in a folder under only a single heading and that relatively non-specific. The type of search that can be conducted effectively in this kind of file is severely limited. Manual files cannot be used effectively in the conduct of highly specific searches or of complex searches involving rela-tionships among several variables. It is this type of search that can be handled rapidly and efficiently in a computer-based retrieval system.

The central system is reasonably comprehensive, nonduplicative, and accessible to all—but it is not *immediately* accessible. Its most severe limitation, however, is the fact that (like all general retrieval systems) it represents a compromise position, being intended to serve the intelligence community in general. A general system of this type does not reflect the specialized interests of any one analyst. There is no "typical" intelligence analyst any more than there is a "typical" medical practitioner. Different analysts have different needs and different viewpoints. It is these specialized viewpoints that the personal files attempt to reflect, although not always successfully, and that the central system cannot cater to very effectively.

Because of these considerations, it is unlikely that in any large organi-zation a central retrieval system will eliminate the need for personal documentation systems. Conversely, personal collections do not eliminate the need for a strong central system. Clearly, some synergy between personal systems and the central system is required, a point made very cogently by Burton and Yerke (1969):

> Many systems analysts and research administrators regard with great skepticism the personal documentation systems which most scientists maintain. These systems are viewed as evidence that the formal bibliographic services pro-vided by the researcher's supporting institution are poorly designed or functioning improperly. Accordingly attention has been focused chiefly on improvement of library services and related bibliographic systems
>
> It is not yet widely understood that personal information systems are necessary to researchers because their orientation is basically antithetical to that of the formal system. The formal system is designed to be objective, inclusive, and normative. It may also tend to become static. The personal system is by definition subjective, heuristic, and dynamic. It provides its user with an information transfer environment dominated by his own viewpoint. He is the favored observer of his information universe. He determines what goes into the system and the relevance of retrieval results. And in this kind of documentation "relevance" is based on ever varying subjective criteria.
>
> Properly understood, both the formal and the personal systems contribute to the satisfaction of information needs by providing complementary services. To

ignore either of the two systems, or to force one to substitute for the other, results in higher cost to the user and a lowering of quality of over-all service [p. 53].[1]

In considering the need for an improved information handling system within the Agency, then, it became increasingly clear that any central system, however efficient, would not eliminate the requirement for some form of personal files. Indeed, it was clearly undesirable to attempt such an action. However, there seemed to be a critical need to improve the organization of personal files, to allow them to be searched more effectively, as well as to reduce these files in bulk. It seemed clear that these large paper copy files, occupying considerable space in the building, could not be allowed to continue to grow indefinitely in their existing form. At the same time, it was obviously necessary to make the central system more accessible and more attractive in order to encourage analysts to use the full range of information resources in preparing finished intelligence.

For many years, personal files were virtually ignored by librarians and other information specialists. Very little research was conducted on their characteristics, such as type of document collected, organization, and use factors. In general, there was a tendency for information professionals to look with disfavor on personal files. Frequently they were regarded as a "necessary evil" which, if ignored, might eventually go away. Since 1960, however, there seems to have occurred an increasing realization that personal files will not disappear, that they have an important function to play in the overall information handling activities of any research organization, and that the information specialist should be concerned with helping individuals to organize their files and to utilize them more effectively. A number of systems have applied data processing capabilities in order to improve the organization, accessibility, and exploitation of personal files. These systems have been developed in government, in the academic world, and in the commercial sector. They include both off-line systems, such as SURF (Support of User Records and Files) (Wallace, 1966) and FAMULUS (Burton and Yerke, 1969), and on-line systems. Examples of on-line systems to support personal files are the RIQS system at Northwestern University (Borman and Mittman, 1972), the AUTONOTE system at the University of Michigan (Reitman *et al.*, 1969), and the Mitre Corporation's SHOEBOX (Glantz, 1970).

These systems help individual scientists or other professionals to organize and exploit their personal files more effectively, allow them to

---

[1] Reprinted by permission of John Wiley & Sons, Inc.

index documents in any way desired, and provide an improved searching capability. The "improved searching capability" varies in sophistication, from the production of machine listings and indexes, and the availability of an off-line search capability, to providing on-line access to the files. For a number of years the SHOEBOX system has been used, in a limited and specialized application, by one of the branches of the Central Intelligence Agency. The apparent success of this application and, indeed, the apparent success of most such systems for providing computer support to personal files, was a significant influence on the conceptualization of the intelligence system that is described later.

Conversion from Off-Line to On-Line Operation

The major impetus behind this conceptualization, however, occurred in 1972 when plans were being made to convert the Agency-wide retrieval system from an off-line, batch processing mode to an on-line mode. There were several reasons why such a conversion appeared necessary. First, the files were becoming too large to be searched efficiently by the serial processing of magnetic tapes. It was becoming necessary to convert to a random access storage device and to an "inverted" form of file organization. There was also a need to provide a system that could be made more generally accessible to intelligence analysts, to encourage increased use, and one that could provide results that were virtually immediate rather than delayed.

At first a somewhat narrow approach was adopted. The main concern was to convert the existing central system from an off-line, serial search mode to an on-line, random access mode of operation. The major emphasis was on the identification of a suitable system for file management and for searching in an on-line, interactive mode.[2] A leading contender was the RECON system of NASA, a system "in the public domain" for which there was a considerable accumulation of experience at NASA and elsewhere. The RECON software had been brought into the Agency and experiments were underway to apply this system in the intelligence environment.

It soon became clear, however, that this approach was a myopic one. Existing problems would not all be solved simply by making the existing data base more accessible on-line. A broader view seemed necessary. In fact, in planning the move to an on-line, interactive system, it seemed highly appropriate to consider the potential impact of on-line processing

---

[2] The central data base was already accessible through on-line terminals but this on-line system had limited capabilities, was cumbersome, and was noninteractive.

on all activities designed to support the information handling activities of the production analyst. The idea then arose of designing a much more ambitious Agency-wide information processing system, one that would help the analyst organize his own files, give him ready access to more general data bases, and even play an important role in document dissemination activities.

Conceptualizing a Paperless System

As a result of the considerations outlined earlier in the chapter a decision was made, late in 1972, to implement a small "model" of a proposed on-line information system for the Agency. The idea was to get a small scale system up and running in order to demonstrate its capabilities to a few pilot branches in the organization, to assess analyst reaction, and to gather data that would be necessary to prepare a more detailed design for a complete system.

The major concern was to develop a system that would give analysts on-line access to their own files and also give them on-line access to the major Agency retrieval systems. It was also considered highly desirable that the analysts should be able to exploit, from the same terminal, a wide range of full text data bases, derived by procedures mentioned earlier. Also considered was the possibility of giving the analyst access to certain "outside" data bases. The whole idea behind this was the creation of a system that would give the user a "widening horizons" approach to an information search, as depicted in Figure 2. From his terminal the user would be able to search files that he himself (or the branch to which he belongs) had created. Having exhausted the resources of personal and/or branch files, the user would then be able to extend his search, from the same terminal and, hopefully, using the same or a similar query language, into other Agency-wide data bases, including the central system and a wide range of text files. Conceivably, he could use the same terminal to search other outside data bases to which the agency had acquired access, such as MEDLINE and the *New York Times* Information Bank.

It was considered that such a system would give the analyst an extremely powerful tool for search and retrieval. From a single terminal, conveniently at hand, a very wide range of resources could be made available to him. These resources would be much more accessible than they had ever been before and the hope was that, by improving their accessibility, they would be exploited more fully and more effectively in the preparation of finished intelligence. Although all the elements depicted in Figure 2 were regarded as important, it was considered that

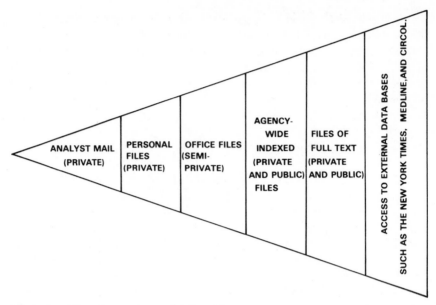

Figure 2. Widening spectrum of information resources available to analyst from his terminal.

the two most valuable features would be (a) access to personal and branch files, and (b) access to full text files.

For reasons discussed earlier, the personal and branch files constitute the most important information source available to the analyst. In the proposed system the analyst would be given the capabilities of his present filing system and much more besides. It was considered extremely important that the system should not impose any artificial constraints on the analyst. He would not be required to learn and apply any particular indexing system. Nor would any thesaurus, classification scheme, or other form of vocabulary control be imposed on him. Instead, he would be completely free to assign any terms he wished to documents. He could, for example, continue to use the file headings that he found convenient in the organization of his paper files; however, no limit would be placed on the number of such headings that could be assigned to a particular item. Moreover, he could supplement these headings by the free assignment of keywords of any type he chose, including place names and names of individuals. By this means he would be given a level of access to his files that had never previously been possible. Not only would access be improved in breadth (because of the number of access points provided) but it would also be improved in depth (because of the specificity of the access points that would be allowed). Thus the analyst would have greatly improved capabilities for searching personal and branch files since he could search on various types of file heading (some representing subject, some geographic region) and on assigned keywords in any combination.

Of course, the files that the analyst would create, and would be able to interrogate on-line, would be different from his manual files in that they would comprise document surrogates rather than full text. It would be necessary to provide him with microform copies of items in his files. A microfilm reader–printer would be made readily accessible to the on-line terminal so that the analyst could go from a search mode to a document recovery mode with a minimum of effort.

The capability of providing on-line access to full text files was also considered to be of great importance. Although analysts had had access to text files before, it was proposed to make these files much more accessible by allowing them to be interrogated from an on-line terminal in the analyst's own office. At the same time, the system would provide access to a much wider range of such files, not only general-purpose files (e.g., all State Department cables for a specified period of time), but also special-purpose files that could be created, possibly from multiple sources, to meet the needs of particular branches. Full text files are considered to have great value because they are complete, in the sense that nothing is eliminated from the documents, and because they can be searched in a very specific way (any word, or combination of words, including names in text, can be searched on). In the intelligence community, where it is sometimes difficult to predict in advance what particular items are worth indexing and what aspects of these items should be indexed, a full text search capability on selected files is of great potential value.

In conceptualizing the prototype system, it was considered necessary to provide more than a searching capability. It would certainly be desirable to give the analyst an on-line file building capability. That is, to provide a feature whereby the analyst, or possibly the analyst's secretary, could index documents at the on-line terminal itself. Fortunately, an on-line indexing capability had already been developed for use with the central system. This on-line indexing capability had been fully tested and evaluated, and was in an operational status. In this on-line input process, an indexing "data form" is displayed on a CRT device. The on-line user completes the form by putting the applicable values into the appropriate fields of the display. The on-line input programs are organized in such a way that they minimize the number of keystrokes that need to be made in order to complete a record. Various error checking and validation operations are also built into the programs. The on-line input technique had been carefully compared with the input procedures in use earlier, namely the preparation of special input forms and the scanning of these by an optical character reading (OCR) device. With skilled typists involved in each case, it was found that the on-line input operation was considerably cheaper than the OCR input, and that it offered other significant advantages, including input of records more rapidly and, with experience, a reduced error rate. It was thought that, with minor modification, the on-line input procedures developed for use with the central system (the technique is referred to as On-Line Data Entry) could also be used by an analyst, or secretary, to build up his own indexed files on-line.

In the early conceptualization, the thinking had mainly been directed toward the provision of file building and file searching capabilities. Later, however, it was recognized that, if terminals were to be widely available to analysts within the Agency, steps should be taken to ensure that these devices would be fully utilized. Other possible uses were therefore considered. An obvious candidate was the dissemination process. Since about 70% of all messages entering the organization are electricals, it was possible to conceive of a system in which dissemination would be carried out not in paper copy form, but by routing of messages to user terminals. The analyst could thus view his daily "mail" on-line. Conceivably, he could also be given various processing capabilities for use with his mail file. For example, he could "destroy" unwanted items, refer items to other analysts, put selected items (in full text form) into a "hold" file, index documents for future retrieval by selecting keywords from text, draw extracts from complete messages, add comments and notes, and store in permanent or semi-permanent files the full text of messages or extracts from them, together with analyst supplied comments or notes.

One last application of the on-line terminals seemed feasible and desirable. That was the provision of an on-line text editing capability so that an analyst, if he chose, could write finished intelligence reports at the terminal, and could route them to other analysts for their information. The on-line editing capabilities would make it easy for the analyst to alter text and add to it at any point. The end result would be a finished report in machine-readable form that would be used as direct input to photocomposition procedures, or indeed, that would be input to the electronic processing stream, thus making this a continuous and regenerative cycle.

Gradually, then, the concept of a largely paperless information system began to emerge, a system in which analysts could receive documents digitally, process these in various ways, build files, search a wide range of personal, branch, and more general files, including full text files, and use the terminal in the actual creation of finished intelligence documents. The system thus conceptualized was named SAFE (Support for the Analyst File Environment).

The Characteristics of a Paperless System for Use in the Intelligence Community

The SAFE system is intended to support approximately 2000 production analysts by providing faster dissemination of intelligence, giving them greater access to personal and community files, and enabling them to produce more timely and thorough intelligence reports. The system should also reduce time and effort involved in paper handling as well as saving document storage space and cost. In the system described, analysts use on-line terminal devices to read their mail, build files, query these files, query other files as appropriate, perform basic data manipulation, and compose intelligence reports.

The system capabilities can be summarized by describing the SAFE Console Station (SCS), the files it can access, and the processes it can perform. The SAFE system, where practical, is to be integrated into the general Agency data processing environment so that a terminal can be used to access other Agency data bases in addition to SAFE files. Figure 3 presents an overview of system capabilities, showing the various categories of files that will be available, as well as the processing functions that can be applied to these files. The user will be able to switch among these various files and processing capabilities at a single terminal session.

Each analyst served will use the system through a SAFE Console Station (SCS) which may consist of a "local" terminal (viewing screen and keyboard), a digital printer close to the terminal, and a "regional" microfilm viewing screen, film storage device, and printer. The keyboards will have function keys that control the file categories to be accessed and the functions to be performed. The SCS will be designed with either two screens or a split screen, so that an analyst can view information on one part while entering data on another.

The capabilities of the system are best considered in terms of the various functions that it will perform for the analysts served. An outline of these functions follows.

DISSEMINATION AND CURRENT AWARENESS

A major distinction must be made between the documents arriving in digital form (*electricals*) and those arriving only in hard copy form. For

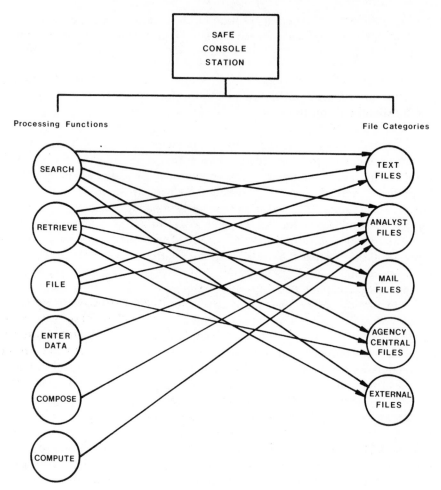

Figure 3.   Overview of SAFE capabilities.

the foreseeable future, the latter will be handled as they are at present; that is, they will be disseminated in multiple paper copies. It is the general strategy, however, to encourage the transmission of an increasing volume of intelligence material in digital form. This will mean that an increasing proportion of everything processed can be handled in the paperless mode described later. It is also conceivable that, at a later time, some of the documents arriving only as paper will be digitized so that the processing of these can be integrated into the paperless flow.

All electrical messages will be disseminated automatically to user terminals on the basis of user interest profiles or by a combination of machine and human activities as described earlier. Dissemination in this case merely means that the documents go into a special text storage file (called the Mail File) and the addressee codes are added to a Master Index Record (MIR) existing in the system. When the analyst goes into a Mail Scan mode, he can view a "status board" which tells how many messages have accumulated for him since he last used the system for current awareness purposes. The analyst can then ask to have these messages displayed. Note, however, that the text of the message is stored only once however many analysts it is addressed to. An analyst's "mail file" consists only of a set of pointers to certain records in the general Mail File.

A message that is of no further interest to an analyst can be disposed of at the touch of a key. "Disposed of" means merely that the analyst's address code for this document is removed from the Master Index Record (MIR). Alternatively, one may wish to re-route a message to another analyst. This may be done by entering the address code for this analyst and including a message to indicate why and from whom it is being sent. The message goes into a Message File, tied to the MIR, so that a document with accompanying message can be delivered to the analyst addressed (i.e., the analyst address code is added to the MIR and a pointer to the Message File is also created there).

A document extract capability also exists in the system. The extract feature forms "windows" of text around words or phrases in which an analyst expresses special interest. That is, if the analyst so chooses, the extract capability can be applied to selected words or word combinations in his interest profile. When he logs into the system, and goes into a Mail Scan Mode, he may request the extract feature. This means that he looks first at the text extracts built for him and goes secondarily to the full documents extracted. The extract feature is intended to save the time of the analyst and to present for his immediate attention those items likely to require the most rapid action on his part. It may therefore be regarded as a kind of ranking capability. The value of this feature is likely to be directly related to the volume of mail received by a particular analyst.

Some form of "priority message" alerting capability is also planned. When the dissemination procedures, human or automatic, detect an incoming document that is a high priority item, requiring immediate action, the normal processing flow is disturbed momentarily to give this message priority treatment. A type of alarm mechanism at the terminal will alert an analyst to the arrival of such an item.

An analyst is likely to go into a Mail Scan mode when he first arrives in the morning and again at selected times during the day. At any time he can use the system "status board" to find how many documents are still in his mail file (i.e., have not been disposed of or directed elsewhere) and how many have arrived since he last used the system. The processes of document receipt and dissemination are, of course, continuous throughout the day. Electronic dissemination can be much more rapid than the paper dissemination that it replaces. It is particularly efficient for the handling of high priority documents.

The Mail File is a temporary file of digital text organized in such a way that it can be searched in a full text mode. That is, a user can go into a text search mode and can search on any word, or combination of words, occurring in the text files. In this way the individual analyst can augment the system's dissemination component. He can check on the system dissemination to be sure that he has not missed any items of importance, and he can also check the Mail File for any new or transient interest that is not reflected in his user interest profile within the dissemination module.

The Mail File will grow very rapidly, however, and it may not prove economical to maintain it in a searchable form for a long period. Moreover, intelligence documents, more so than any other type of document, tend to obsolesce very rapidly. The peak of interest in the majority of these documents is likely to be measurable in hours or, at the most, days from the time of arrival in the organization. Thereafter, the interest is likely to decline. This does not mean that they will never be used again, but merely that the overall probability of use, for the majority of documents, will decline with age. It is quite reasonable, therefore, that documents should be retired to successively less accessible files in the system on the basis of age and measures of their activity. The life of the Mail File, then, is likely to be one of days rather than months. In other words, the full text of a document will be searchable in the Mail File for a specified period of time after its receipt. After that, the text could be retired to a secondary level of access. It could, for example, go into a digital text file from which documents can be retrieved by means of various indicators in the MIR, but in which it will no longer be possible to conduct a full text search. Some items, however, could be retired from the Mail File directly to microform via computer-output microfilm (COM) procedures. This would apply most clearly to certain documents of a routine, administrative nature whose continued intelligence value is likely to be low.

An analyst who, on viewing a document that has been transmitted to him or found by a search in the Mail File, wishes to retain the item for permanent reference, must add the document to his own files. This activity is described next.

FILE BUILDING

On-line indexing capabilities are available to allow an analyst to create and index his own document files. The analyst can call up an on-line for-matted display into which he inserts the "values" he wishes to use for indexing purposes. An automatic "citation generation program" will already have cataloged the item. This means that, when the analyst calls up an indexing form by the number automatically assigned to the docu-ment in the system, he will already find certain standard data present. These standard cataloging data include such items as document title, source, destination, date, and security classification. The analyst is allowed to index a document, for his own future retrieval purposes, in absolutely any way he wishes. He may use keywords and any type of subject or geographic coding scheme he prefers. The system thus gives him all the retrieval capabilities of paper files, plus very much more besides. Any retrieval tags he chooses to use will be pointers to the document in the system. These retrieval approaches will be his own. No other person may use them without specific authorization to access his files. The same document, then, although physically existing in the system only once, can be "present" in the files of, say 20 different analysts and, in each of these files, be indexed in completely different ways to represent specialized needs and viewpoints.

The analyst can index a hard copy document in much the same way that he indexes an electrical. That is, he calls up a form by document number and enters his retrieval tags for the item. In this case the docu-ment will be stored in the system as a microform rather than as a digital record.

When the system is fully implemented, the analyst will have much greater on-line indexing sophistication than now exists. He is likely to have a dual screen display, allowing him to view digital text on one screen and the indexing format on the other. He will also have the capability of mark-ing certain words in the text (e.g., by a light pen) and transferring these to the indexing record without the need for re-keying.

If an analyst is interested in only a certain portion of a long document, he may "extract" this portion for storage in his own files. This capability, in the case of electricals, means that the index terms in his file point not to the complete document but to a designated portion of it only (e.g., a certain paragraph). In some cases too, the analyst may have evaluated a document and made comments on it. The system gives him the capability of storing these comments. They will go into a Comments File, tied to the document text itself by the MIR, so that he may call up docu-ment and comments for simultaneous viewing on his screen.

The integrated electronic system does not preclude the need for a central Agency-wide retrieval system. A certain proportion of all documents entering the Agency (those series or sources deemed of the highest intelligence value) will continue to be indexed into this "central" system. They will be indexed by information specialists, using keywords plus standard subject and geographic codes, in much the same way that an analyst indexes a document into his own files. In this case, however, the access points provided become "public access points", by which any user can retrieve the document, restricted only by security limitations imposed on the document and/or individual.

DOCUMENT STORAGE

It is now necessary to look at the various file components that have been mentioned and to consider how they are related. This is best done by an examination of Figure 4, which gives a somewhat simplified picture of the overall structure of the files but is sufficient for our present purposes. The key to the entire system is the Master Index Record (MIR) File, for it is this file that ties all the others together. Each document in

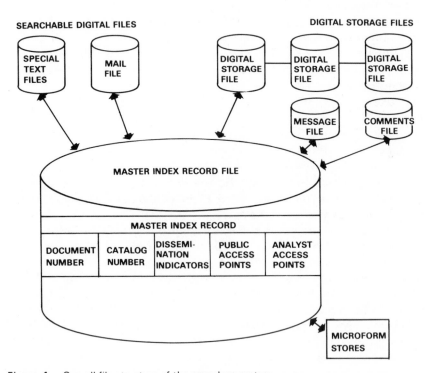

Figure 4.   Overall file structure of the paperless system.

the system is given a unique number (automatically assigned), by which the MIR, or selected portions of it, can be retrieved. The MIR for a document will include at least a minimal catalog record. It may also include dissemination indicators (i.e., codes for individuals or offices to whom the item was sent), public access points (if the item has been indexed into the central system), and analyst access points (if it has been added to one or more personal files).

The dissemination indicators give an analyst access to any documents, bearing his own code, present in the Mail File. These indicators will disappear when a document is removed from the Mail File, although they may be stored elsewhere as a historical record of who received what. An analyst may also retrieve a document through the public access points and through his own access points (assuming he has added it to his files) but may not retrieve it through terms assigned by any other analyst. As mentioned earlier, an important principle of the system is that a document should be stored only once even though it may appear to exist in a number of different files.

Besides the MIR file, there are three other types of files depicted in Figure 4. Whereas the MIR file consists only of document representations, the other files all contain the full text of documents. They consist of searchable digital files, digital storage files, and microform stores. The searchable digital files are self-explanatory. They are files so structured that they can be directly interrogated, in a full text search mode, from an on-line terminal. The Mail File we have already mentioned. The Special Text Files are files built for special purposes. These files might include all documents of a particular type (e.g., selected series of high intelligence value) as well as files built on particular subjects of great current interest. This latter type of file, which would include documents arriving electrically from many different sources, can be created completely automatically as a by-product of the dissemination system. This means that an interest profile is created for the file, rather than for an office or individual analyst, and documents matching the profile are read-off into the special text files. Under certain circumstances, special files of this type might be built for different departments, or even individual analysts, where the subject matter is one of great current concern.

The digital storage files are like the searchable digital files in that they contain the full text of documents. The difference is that the former are not directly searchable in a full text mode. Specific items in these files can be retrieved only by document number (i.e., they are document delivery systems in digital form). When an analyst conducts a search in the MIR file, using various combinations of index terms or other identifiers, he is told by the system whether the documents that match his strategy are in digital form or microform. If in digital form, they can be displayed at his terminal, in whichever digital file (digital storage file, Mail File, Special Text Files) they happen to appear. In the case of access through the dissemination indicators or analyst access points, the MIR may also point to related items in the Message File or the Comments File. Thus, when an analyst asks to see certain documents, these will be displayed along with appropriate messages, from another analyst, or comments that he himself has made.

The full text search capabilities of the system are greatly extended by a "stringsearch" capability. A user can reduce a search to a manageable number of items (say several hundred) in any file through the use of the MIR file, have these read into a "workspace," and then go into a text search mode on these items.

Finally, we have the microform stores. These, again, are not searchable files but document delivery systems. Any item arriving only as paper copy will go into the microform stores. These stores may also contain some items that once existed digitally but, because of low probability of future use, have been retired to a less accessible and less costly storage medium. At the present stage of system development, these microforms are divided among a central microform store and a series of local stores that correspond to the paper files maintained by an individual or a department. The analyst must physically retrieve a microfiche and manually insert it into a microfiche viewer. At a later stage of system implementation, however, automatic retrieval of microfiche (from one central store or a series of regional stores) is seen to be necessary. In this case the retrieved item will be transmitted for display at the analyst's viewing station on the same screen that he uses to conduct his search, or possibly an adjacent screen used only for microimage viewing. When this stage of development is reached, the analyst can view any document in complete form at his terminal whether it exists within the system as a digital record or as a microform.

It is clear that the three types of document files reflect priorities in the system. The documents that are of greatest current interest are in the searchable digital files (although still potentially accessible through index terms or other tags in the MIR file), while those of lesser current interest are in the digital storage files, and the least currently significant items (of those that arrived electrically at least) are in the microform stores. The principle of "age/activity file reorganization" is important in the overall system design. Age/activity reorganization implies that records are retired to successively less accessible storage areas depending on their age and the amount of use they have received. Use of each record is recorded as part of system monitoring activities (discussed later in this chapter), a count being updated each time the record is accessed through the MIR. Even within the digital storage files there may exist differential levels of accessibility.

The dispersion of documents throughout these various files is at least partly a matter of economics. As increasingly efficient and less expensive mass storage devices with rapid access capabilities are developed, it is likely that more and more of the complete data base will exist digitally and files of greater size will be retained in searchable digital form. With further developments that will allow the capture of more and more documents in digital form (e.g., the acquisition of machine-readable newspapers), together with the possibility of developing less costly procedures for digitizing other printed items, it is likely that the microform component in the system will gradually become less important. It is worth noting, however, that there are some types of documents that cannot now be handled well in the electronic mode or, for that matter, in microform. One example is the high-quality aerial reconaissance photograph. For the immediately foreseeable future, such items will still need to be given special treatment. They form a very small percentage, however, of all the documents processed.

Before leaving Figure 4 completely, it is worth emphasizing that this diagram gives simply a general indication of system file structure. No particular form of file organization or, for that matter, storage medium should be inferred. Moreover, the several files that are shown as units in the diagram could conceivably be segmented in many different ways. Even the Master Index Record need not necessarily exist as a single unit record, as depicted in the diagram, but may be a set of linked sub-units in various parts of the overall file structure.

SEARCH AND RETRIEVAL

Most of the search and retrieval functions of the system have already been mentioned. The analyst user has access to two types of files: text files and files of document index records. Both types of files can be searched in an on-line, interactive mode. The major search possibilities were illustrated in Figure 2. The analyst may search his own mail file (or indeed, the complete Mail File, subject to security restrictions) and his own indexes. He may extend a search into "office files" or to various types of Agency-wide files in indexed and full text form. "Office files" refers to files maintained by a particular section for the use of all analysts in the section. In principle they are no different from the personal files. In some sections all files may be maintained by individuals, in others a file may serve a group of individuals with closely related interests, while in yet others the section may be served by a combination of office and individual files.

It is also intended that the system allow analysts access to various data bases outside the Agency (e.g., CIRCOL, MEDLINE, the *New York Times* Information Bank). However, the analyst will not necessarily interrogate these data bases directly from his terminal. Instead, there will exist a terminal room in which are located a number of terminals, accessing external data bases, manned by information specialists skilled in the searching of one or more of these systems. The individual analyst may use his terminal to communicate with the trained searchers in this information facility. Thus his terminal gives him access to these particular data bases through information specialists acting as intermediaries. The terminals can be used to maintain a dialog, for the purpose of clarifying an information need, between the analysts and the information specialists. There are certain advantages to this mode of operation. First, while an analyst is likely to use the internal information resources frequently, and will thus learn how to exploit these files effectively, he will probably not consult any one external source on a regular basis. Consequently, he would be at a great disadvantage in trying to search a data base about which he knows rather little. In this case the information specialist, who is well acquainted with a few external files, is likely to do a better job of searching for the analyst than he would be able to do himself. The second advantage relates to ease of implementation. Each of these external systems has its own language of interrogation. It would be unrealistic to expect each intelligence analyst to learn six or seven such languages in order to make relatively infrequent use of these sources. The alternative to this would be the design of some form of switching language which would accept a query in a standard format and convert it to the language of any of the available external systems. While such a device could be created, the problems involved are by no means trivial. The third and final advantage relates to system security. It is easier to ensure complete security of the system if the SAFE terminals themselves do not access external data bases directly through regular telephone lines.

In the exploitation of external data bases it is likely that some form of referral data base will be needed. Such a data base would incorporate a detailed index to the characteristics of the various external data bases. Perhaps it will go so far as to include the entire vocabularies of these data bases. An analyst may input a statement of information need and request that it be matched against this referral file. This device will then indicate the probability that an external data base will include items relevant to the request. In fact, it may go further and rank the external data bases in order of their probable utility for a particular search. Such a ranking can be achieved by a fairly simple algorithm that matches the characteristics of the statement of information need with the characteristics of the various data bases. The concept of a referral data base is illustrated in more detail in Chapter 8.

SPECIAL PROCESSING FUNCTIONS

There are some additional system capabilities that have not yet been mentioned. One of these is the "compute" function. The analyst has available to him various computational and statistical manipulation programs. He can apply these programs to any documents in the system that contain numerical data. In fact, although the above description generally assumed files of documents, some of the analyst files may be files of data rather than files of text.

The system may also be used for various forms of interanalyst communication. This means that the terminal will put an analyst in touch with any other analyst for the routing and rerouting of documents, drafts, and other messages.

DOCUMENT COMPOSITION

Analysts will use their consoles to pull together information relevant to a proposed intelligence report or memorandum. For this they will use the search and retrieval function and/or the computational capabilities of the system. Conceivably, an analyst will create a special project file in anticipation of a forthcoming intelligence report requirement. As he prepares to write the piece, he might choose to retrieve all the records within this file. He might display all of the comments that he entered during file building. After viewing them, he might wish to edit by adding or deleting. He might also wish to review whole items and extract parts with or without additional comments. He can search public files for recently added information and, if he finds something relevant to his problem, he may add it, with or without comments, to his file.

Analysts will also have the option of utilizing the numerical processing function when preparing intelligence reports. Conceivably, there will be data present in a special file that a user wishes to present in some unique way. He can derive certain values from these data by performing various computations and have the results displayed at his console or printed off-line.

As a result of the above activities, the analyst should have in front of him all the relevant materials that are available from the SAFE system and can now complete his intelligence report. Finished intelligence items can be composed, edited, and printed at the SAFE console. On-line composition and text editing procedures are available to aid this task. Output so produced would be suitable for actual submission, whether in electrical or paper form (produced, for example, by photocomposition). The finished intelligence item is now available in machine form as the result of the production method, and can be treated as an incoming item and processed accordingly. It will be cataloged, indexed for distribution, disseminated, filed, and so on. The system may thus be regarded as continuous and regenerative.

MANAGEMENT AND MONITORING

In a system of the size and complexity of the one described, it is imperative that an efficient monitoring subsystem should exist to record the type and time of occurrence of each significant event in use of the system. The design of monitors for on-line retrieval systems has been discussed in the literature by Mittman and Dominick (1973).

Essentially the on-line monitor will incorporate four major components:

1. An information management system to record and log all activities for which data are needed for management purposes
2. A system to store the logged data in a prescribed format and to allow selected data to be retrieved on demand
3. A statistical program to allow the analysis of these data
4. A graphics package that will allow the presentation of certain data in the form of plots, on paper or at a terminal

The monitoring operation will be designed to collect data for the following purposes: (a) for management control and reporting; (b) to ensure the efficient utilization of system resources; (c) to collect data needed for the age/activity reorganization of the files; (d) for diagnostic purposes—to identify system problems that need to be corrected in order that performance may be improved; and (e) to monitor the reliability of the system and its components.

To achieve these goals, data will be collected on: aggregate system usage by time of day and mode of use, volume and type of use by terminal, volume and type of use by user identity, file size and usage, file characteristics (e.g., distribution by size of records, date, number of access points, security classification), use of index terms in indexing and searching, distribution of use of commands, use of synonym tables and other searching aids, number of documents disseminated (number of recipients per document, number of documents per disseminee), interter-

minal communication, system response times, use of each individual
record in the system when accessed through the MIR, clock time and CP
time for all system activities (and thereby unit cost figures for various
operations), user errors as identified by analysis of error messages, use of
system explanations and HELP commands, software malfunctions,
failures at any level of the hardware configuration and the effect of these
on response time.

Evaluation of the Prototype

The complete processing system, as described here, does not yet
exist. However, all the major capabilities have been demonstrated in a
prototype system and this prototype has been thoroughly evaluated. The
analysts themselves were intimately involved in the design of the prototype as well as in the evaluation activities. Perhaps the most significant
element in the SAFE design philosophy was the recognition, from the
beginning of the project, that representatives of the user population must
be directly involved in the design and that a system imposed on these
users from outside, whatever its other merits, is almost certainly doomed
to failure. Design and implementation of the prototype, then, involved
continuous and intensive contact with designated representatives in the
various user offices. These users commented on design proposals,
experimented with new features as they were added to the system, and
criticized these in a constructive fashion, leading to modifications in the
design. The prototype was therefore as user-oriented as it was possible
to make it.

In the prototype evaluation a number of test "modules," representing
the major capabilities of the proposed system, were implemented and
demonstrated to a number of offices within the Agency—offices that had
expressed immediate interest in SAFE and, perhaps more importantly, a
willingness to volunteer the use of their time and their files. Most of the
data collection was carried out with four of these "pilot branches,"
although as many as 30 branches and over 100 analysts were involved
in some aspect of the system in this phase, which occupied the period
from late 1973 to the summer of 1974.

Each of various modules used in the evaluation represented a specific
information processing capability and a specific intelligence resource.
Each of these modules either already existed in 1973 or could be
demonstrated with a minimum of resources. The first working
demonstrations were given at a single central terminal. Later, CRT display devices, printers, and microfilm viewers were installed in a number

of the pilot branches. This equipment constituted a prototype SAFE Console Station. Analysts suggested improvements as they worked with the various modules during the test period. Some of these improvements were incorporated into the system during the test period itself; others will be incorporated into the final system design.

The testing of the various modules required the use of several computer programs either in existence or in the development stage. The machine-aided dissemination system (MAD) permitted the building of special files of cables and other electricals for the pilot branches; the Agency-wide retrieval system allowed analysts to tap directly on-line into various subsets of the central files; and OLDE (On-line Data Entry) could be used to allow analysts to build computer searchable files by entering data at their consoles. At a later stage of the prototype, the RECON software was adopted to provide interactive searching capabilities.

Early in 1973 work was begun on the development of software to allow analysts to search, on their SAFE terminals, the full text of special files of cables and other electricals. The program was completed by the end of 1973. In 1973, too, a "data extract" program was implemented. This program allows analysts to search the full text of messages for specific words and, when the words are located, to extract a specific segment of the message. For example, an analyst could specify that each time a certain name was found in a cable, he wanted to see the title of that cable, with the option of seeing the whole cable if necessary.

In 1974 three "on-line text analysis" programs were implemented. The first version allowed an analyst to scan and "file" his electrical mail (those items disseminated by the MAD system) on his SAFE terminal. The second version allowed the segments found by the "data extract" program to be viewed as mail and the whole message to be viewed on demand. The final version allowed analysts to interact more completely with their mail—they could add index terms and comments, extract portions of a message for their files, and edit messages before filing them.

The prototype system, with modules for dissemination/current awareness, text search, on-line search of personal and central files, and file-building, was made available in a "pilot" or "data gathering" mode with the following objectives:

1. To determine the attitudes of analysts toward SAFE in general and to the various separate features it provides
2. To determine how useful a system of this type would be to production analysts
3. To collect the data needed in order to move the system beyond the experimental and into a more fully operational mode

For this last purpose, a vast quantity of data was collected on how the prototype was used, how frequently, with what degree of success, what its failures and limitations were, what features analysts would need in an expanded system, volumes of documents, numbers of searches, times involved, and so on.

Extensive studies of user reaction to the prototype indicated a strong commitment to the concept of a paperless system and a desire to see the pilot develop into a fully operational system of greater scope, sophistication, and reliability. It is interesting to note that the advantages claimed were the advantages, presented earlier, that were anticipated by the designers of the system before it was ever implemented, namely: (a) material available more rapidly; (b) a level of access to material never previously possible; (c) saving of space and paper handling; and (d) the ability of an analyst to extend a search for information over many different files so that he could "bring more evidence to bear on a given problem." Particularly significant was the recognition that the system could have an important role to play in "crisis management." Even in its prototype form, SAFE was able to contribute to keeping analysts abreast of current developments in a crisis situation. The mail handling, message saving, and full text search capabilities of the system make it potentially of great value during crisis situations.

The major purpose of the evaluation activities was to determine if computers could assist intelligence analysts by providing faster dissemination of intelligence materials, giving them greater access to personal and community files, and enabling them to produce more timely and thorough intelligence reports. To conduct the experiment, a rather imperfect representation of the "ideal" system was created. A low-cost package of hardware and software was assembled for test purposes, and the entire data gathering phase was plagued, particularly in its early days, with problems of system availability and reliability. Moreover, the system was very unstable in this phase of its development in that changes were frequently being made (including major changes related to query language) and new capabilities were constantly being added.

In view of the imperfection of the system, the fact that it was in a constant state of flux, and its lack of reliability, the results of the experiment seemed very promising indeed. Although not all analysts in the participating branches used the system extensively, those who did were generally extremely positive in their reactions. There appeared to be much less resistance to a "paperless" operation than might have been expected when the experiment began. Indeed, the whole concept was received with considerable enthusiasm. It is clear that several branches became heavily dependent upon the experimental system, that even in its imperfect form it was able to make a contribution to intelligence production, and that several of the participating branches became sufficiently dependent on SAFE to be seriously handicapped were it to be withdrawn.

There was evidence that all the tested features have definite utility but, as might be expected, different analysts regarded different features as being of greatest importance. It seems clear, however, that the really key features are those giving rapid and in-depth access to the complete text of messages or message extracts, together with the features that give a branch the capability of organizing and searching its own files at a level of specificity or complexity that has never previously been possible. In its experimental phase, the system was sometimes used in just the way the designers hoped: a "widening horizons" approach in which a search for information was conducted over several available files.

The data gathering phase of the project must be judged extremely successful for a number of reasons. First, the feasibility of a system of this type was clearly demonstrated in an operational environment. Second, user reaction was quite positive and frequently enthusiastic. Third, the potential value of such a system in intelligence activities was proved, at least in a preliminary way. Fourth, and in some ways most important of all, the study gave a fairly clear picture (from all the accumulated data and surveys of user reaction) of what an "ultimate" system must look like. The implementation of such a system on a wide scale is an expensive undertaking. However, there is considerable evidence to suggest that the system could make a very significant contribution to the work of the Agency. By having access to intelligence materials more rapidly than ever before, by having immediate access to an extremely wide range of such materials, and by having the capability of searching these materials at levels of specificity and complexity never previously possible, the conscientious analyst will be better informed than in the past. Improved intelligence production must inevitably result.

Present Status of the System

In May 1977 the Central Intelligence Agency issued a Request for Proposal for the "design competition phase" of SAFE. In this phase of system development, two contractors have been selected to perform concurrent design studies of approximately one year's duration. One of these two contractors will then be selected to perform the "system acquisition phase" (i.e., implement the full system). The full system is expected to be operational by 1981.

No description of the hardware configuration needed to implement the full system has been given. This is deliberate for, while the design is fairly firm in terms of what the system is to do, it is not at all firm in terms of how the functions are to be carried out. One possible configuration would be a distributed network of minicomputers, for local processing, attached to general purpose computers doing central processing, but this is only one of several possibilities.

It is recognized that the design and implementation of the full system will present formidable problems. The designers are already well aware of many of these problems, and others will undoubtedly surface as the detailed design progresses. In the volume of documents to be processed for dissemination (several thousand a day), in the size and multiplicity of the files that will be accommodated, in the number of terminals that must be supported in concurrent use, in the complexity of the file organization and reorganization, and in the requirements for very rapid response from certain of the files, the system is larger and more sophisticated than any dissemination and retrieval system now in existence.

Besides its inherent size and complexity, however, the system presents other significant problems in design and implementation. One of these relates to the security of the system. Much of the material handled is of a highly sensitive nature. It is imperative that the system be fully secure. Not only must the files be completely safe from intrusion from outside the Agency, but the files created by one analyst must also be protected from unauthorized access by any other individual. The security problems posed by these requirements are not insuperable; neither are they insignificant.

There is another danger that must be guarded against. SAFE will become an integral part of the working environment of the intelligence analyst. If the system were to break down for any lengthy period of time, the work of many analysts could virtually grind to a halt. System reliability and backup considerations are therefore quite critical. It is intended that the system be designed in such a way that, barring a complete catastrophe, it cannot go down completely. The minicomputer network approach would allow as much processing as possible to be carried out "locally," i.e., close to the analysts. The breakdown of a minicomputer would not affect the whole operation but only a part of it, and that for only a very short time. Such a distributed network might also include several "uncommitted" minicomputers that could be plugged into the network as needed to replace malfunctioning equipment. Likewise, several mainframe computers might be needed to provide adequate backup in the area of central processing. If one went down completely, the system would not collapse, although performance (e.g., in terms of response time) would likely be degraded. As an additional safeguard, various parts of the network, and especially the mainframe computers, could be put on different sources of power. In the event of a power failure, short of something completely catastrophic, the network would be degraded but would not go down completely.

It should be obvious that a system of this kind will not be inexpensive to implement and to maintain. It represents, in fact, a multimillion dollar investment. Can such a system be justified by cost–benefit analysis? What *are* the benefits? First, it must be recognized that part of the investment in this system will be recouped by tangible and substantial savings in other activities. There is a considerable cost involved in generating and distributing many millions of paper copies of documents annually within the Agency. Much of this paper is generated and handled purely to satisfy the distribution function. Many thousands of copies are destroyed within days of being generated, their utility having expired. Even the disposal of these paper copies is not a trivial task. Since most of the messages are highly classified, quite elaborate security precautions are involved in their destruction. The generation of millions of copies of documents and the subsequent human handling involved in moving these copies through the organization, into files, or through destruction routines, represents a very significant annual investment in itself. Much of this paper blizzard will be eliminated by the electronic system.

The paper files of documents that are now maintained within the many branches of the Agency also represent substantial costs. These files are duplicative and extremely space consuming, and space is itself expensive. Not only are these files inefficient, for reasons discussed earlier, but they are also costly to maintain. Filing and refiling of paper copies consumes a vast amount of time daily when considered on an organization-wide basis. Retrieval from the paper files is even more time consuming. Much of this cost will be absorbed by SAFE. Paper will not disappear overnight. But the present paper copy files cannot continue to grow unchecked, consuming space voraciously as they do. Eventually they will disappear. As to the duplication of documents, the electronic system may not eliminate this completely but it will certainly reduce it very considerably. Moreover, the SAFE document files will not be paper copy files. They will be digital files (which *will* be largely files in which a document or record appears only once however many analysts put their "tags" on it) and microform files, the latter possibly in the form of ultramicrofiche. Such files offer major economies in space.

There are further tangible savings that will result from the new system. It will replace several existing systems that are themselves expensive and, in some cases, underutilized. These systems already represent a major investment in machine and human resources. The new system will replace or absorb many of these more or less disconnected activities. The multipurpose character of SAFE, in which many document processing functions will be integrated rather than handled by separate systems, will mean a more coordinated and efficient use of computer resources in the organization as a whole.

Some savings of a less tangible nature are also likely. When fully developed, SAFE should be a highly efficient, sophisticated, and flexible tool that could in the long run save intelligence analysts much time in processing their mail, in building files, in retrieving from files, and in the actual production of intelligence documents.

The electronic system should not, however, be justified on the grounds of cost savings, but rather in terms of its considerable benefits. The system will put in the hands of the intelligence analyst a tool vastly more powerful than any available to him at the present time. It will disseminate messages to him more rapidly. It will give him greatly improved file building capabilities and access to the files he builds. It will give access to a vast array of intelligence resources within the Agency and outside it, and the analyst can search these more completely, more rapidly, and more conveniently than ever before. Furthermore, it will give the analyst analytical capabilities and intelligence production capabilities that are greatly superior to those that now exist.

The justification for SAFE, then, is not merely the elimination of paper. An information handling system that is largely paperless is an interesting phenomenon but not one that is necessarily desirable or justifiable in itself. It has been demonstrated, however, that the system described, and tested as a prototype, has the potential for keeping a major segment of the intelligence community more thoroughly and more swiftly informed than ever before on current developments and on significant events documented in the accumulated literature of the past. A more thoroughly and swiftly informed intelligence community is likely to produce improved intelligence analysis and reporting which, in turn, could have a significant impact on problem solving and decision making at the highest levels.

4

Communication in
Science and Technology

It is now necessary to consider the possibility of implementing a paperless system at a more general level, in the field of science and technology, as suggested in the quotation from the National Science Foundation given in Chapter 1. This statement strongly suggested that we have already reached the limits of print-on-paper systems and that future improvements in communication will depend on our ability to find a viable alternative. The most obvious difference between the intelligence field and the field of science and technology, from the point of view of implementing a paperless system, is that in the former a high percentage of all documents is already created and transmitted electrically, but very little primary publication in this form occurs in the scientific–technical field.

Formal Communication

Before discussing the possibility of paperless systems in science and technology, it seems appropriate to examine the present processes of communication in this field, at least at a general level. Communication can be classified in a number of different ways. One useful classification is a dichotomous division into *formal communication* and *informal communication*, which corresponds roughly to a division into written communication and oral communication. Formal communication is mostly communication by means of documents, usually documents in some type of printed form, whereas informal communication is mostly communication through conversations, face to face or by telephone. Formal communication is impersonal, whereas informal communication is not. White (1971) has also referred to informal communication as *interactive*; it involves a direct interaction between the information source and the recipient of the information. Formal communication, however, is *noninteractive*. The formal–informal and the written–oral divisions do not coincide exactly. Correspondence is a written form of communication, but most people would regard this mode of information transfer as informal rather than formal. The professional conference is in a special category. It is formal in the sense that it involves formal organization and, usually the presentation of formal papers. It will frequently result in some formal publication. It is informal in the sense that much of its value derives from the opportunity it provides for personal communication among individuals who are all working in the same general field. The significance of the conference in scientific communication has been fully discussed in a report from Johns Hopkins University (1970).

Let us look at the formal communication mechanisms first. This is perhaps best done by an examination of Figure 5, which illustrates the major steps involved in the transfer of information through published documents. Research and development activities (using R&D in a very broad sense) lead to new findings, theories, and hypotheses that need to be reported to the scientific community. They are written down in a form suitable for publication. This function, writing, is the role of the author in the communication cycle. At this stage, however, the work of the author has little or no impact on the scientific community. It makes its impact when it is reproduced in multiple copies and distributed in a formal manner (i.e., when it is *published*), which is the role of the primary publisher in the communication cycle. A primary publication, one that contains original compositions, may be a book, a journal, a technical report, a dissertation, a patent, and so on. In science the journal is usually considered to be the major mechanism of formal communication

In Figure 5 primary publications are shown to be distributed in two ways:

1. Directly to the user community through subscription and purchase by individuals
2. Indirectly to the user community through subscription and purchase by libraries and other types of information centers

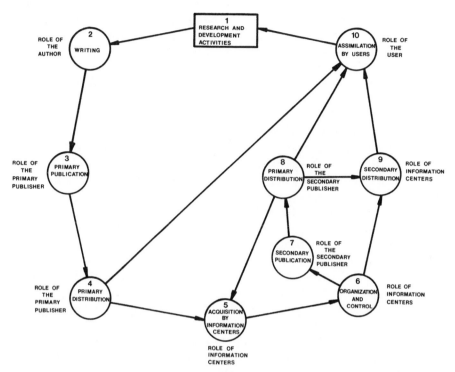

Figure 5. Dissemination of scientific and technical information through primary and secondary publications.

Information centers (this term is used generically in Figure 5 to represent libraries, other kinds of information centers, and the publishers of secondary services) have very important roles to play in the information transfer cycle. Through their acquisition and storage policies, libraries provide a permanent archive of scientific achievement and a guaranteed source of access to this record. In addition, libraries, and other information centers, organize and control the scientific literature by means of cataloging, classification, indexing, and related procedures. Another major role in organization and control is played by the great indexing and abstracting services and by the publishers of national bibliographies. These organizations are responsible for the publication and distribution of *secondary publications*, that is, publications that are guides to the primary literature. Some secondary publications may go directly to the user community. The great majority, however, go to institutional subscribers (i.e., information centers) rather than to individuals.

Information centers also have "presentation and dissemination" functions in the cycle. These functions, which constitute a form of secondary distribution of publications and information about publications, include circulation of materials as well as various types of current awareness, reference, and literature searching services. As specified in Chapter 2, the machine-readable data bases of the secondary publishers are playing an increasingly important role in the provision of various types of information service.

The final stage in the cycle, as shown in Figure 5, is that of assimilation. This, the least tangible, is the stage at which information is absorbed by the scientific community. Here a distinction is being made between *document transfer* and *information transfer*. The latter occurs only if a document is studied by a user and its contents are assimilated to the point at which the reader is *informed* by it (i.e., his state of knowledge on its subject matter is altered). Assimilation of information by the scientific community may occur through primary distribution or secondary distribution. Different documents will have different levels and speeds of assimilation associated with them, and some may never be assimilated at all, because they are never used. One possible measure of assimilation is the extent to which a publication is cited by later writers.

The processes of formal communication are presented as a cycle because they are continuous and regenerative. Through the process of assimilation, readers may gain information that they can use in their own research and development activities. These activities, in turn, generate new writing and publication, and so the cycle continues.

The importance of this communication cycle can hardly be overemphasized. Economic, social, and industrial progress are all dependent on scientific discovery and technological invention. These, in turn, depend heavily on the ability of the science community to assimilate the results of previous research, since modern science is a social activity in which progress is made through group endeavor and a process of gradual accretion, one group building on the work of another. But the results and interpretation of completed research can only be assimilated by the science community if they are properly reported and the reports efficiently disseminated throughout the community. Authors, publishers, librarians, information scientists, indexers, abstractors, and many other individuals, all play very important roles in this communication cycle. A breakdown in the cycle could have very serious consequences. Science itself would stagnate if its own achievements were not efficiently reported, disseminated, and assimilated.

Figure 5 is oversimplified in one important respect. It shows the dissemination of information through formal channels but does not explicitly illustrate the processes of informal communication. The informal channels do not generally disseminate information different from that transferred through the formal channels. Both disseminate the results of the same scientific research. The informal channels differ from the formal channels in that they spread information in a different format or in the same format but at a much earlier time (as, e.g., in the distribution of drafts or preprints). The informal channels are important because they disseminate information more rapidly than the formal channels, at least to those well integrated within the science community, and because they transfer information to some individuals who, for one reason or another, choose not to use the formal channels.

Computers have so far had more impact on secondary publications than on primary publications. Whereas it is probably true to say that the majority of secondary publications are generated from machine-readable data bases, comparatively few primary publications are produced in this way. Moreover, even in secondary publication the machine-readable data base is still viewed primarily as a source from which printed tools can be generated. The machine-readable data base is available for distribution and use but is an alternative to the printed indexing and abstracting publications rather than a replacement for them. That is, apart from a few highly specialized exceptions, there are no secondary publications and no primary publications that exist solely in machine-readable form in the field of science and technology. The exceptions are a few files of numerical or scientific data (rather than documents or document representations) for which no printed analog exists. These files may be termed *data banks*, reserving the term *data bases* for files of a bibliographic nature (i.e., containing documents or document surrogates).

It is clear that paperless communication in science and technology implies the generation of all publications, primary and secondary, in digital form. In fact, it implies that all of the functions of Figure 5 will be handled by an electronic system. How this may occur, and what problems may be involved, will be investigated in later chapters. In the meantime, we should give a little more consideration to present information gathering practices in the scientific community.

Informal Communication

It has been found in a number of studies, conducted over the last 25 years, that scientists and other professionals use many information sources to support their own research and related activities. Some of these are formal sources, whereas others are informal. A number of investigators have studied the variety of information sources used by various categories of professionals and have attempted to identify the factors that determine which source will be used for different types of information need. It has been shown that one very important factor is the stage reached in a particular research project. An investigator is likely to need different types of information at various stages in his or her research and may go to different sources for each type.

Garvey and Griffith (1964), in studying psychologists, found that formal and informal sources are used in the early stages of a project to obtain ideas and to clarify problem areas. Information gathering was considered most important, however, in the later stages of a project, especially in the interpretation of research data. Informal channels are most important in this final stage of the project because other scientists may be needed to aid in the interpretation of the research results. Rees *et al.* (1967) identified three major stages of research. The first draws upon more general background information, the second on specific and factual information, and the third on both general and specific sources. Bertram (1970) studied the relationship between research stage and type of information needed through an analysis of the citations made in various sections of journal articles in chemistry. In the introductory part of the article, references were usually made to complete papers; in the results and discussion section, to parts of other papers; and in the section discussing experimental methods, the references were frequently to specific data in the cited article.

Allen (1966) investigated scientists and engineers on research and development teams. He discovered that the scientists used formal channels more than informal channels throughout the life of a project, whereas the engineers used informal channels much more than formal channels. In both groups, the intensity of the information gathering behavior varied from one stage of a project to another. The relative use of formal and informal channels also varied with research stage.

White (1971) related research stage to the information gathering behavior of academic economists. She identified seven "information functions" in the information exchange behavior of academic economists and found these functions to be quite similar to the types of information needs of research workers identified by earlier investigators, notably Hertz and Rubenstein (1954) and Egan and Henkle (1956). In Table 2, White's information functions are related to the information needs identified by these earlier writers. White was able to suggest several variables affecting the communication behavior of a particular field. One important variable is the purposiveness of the researcher in seeking information.

It has become increasingly evident in the last few years that informal communication is extremely important in science and technology. This

TABLE 2

Relationship of Information Functions to Information Needs as Discussed by Three Investigators of Information-Seeking Behavior[a]

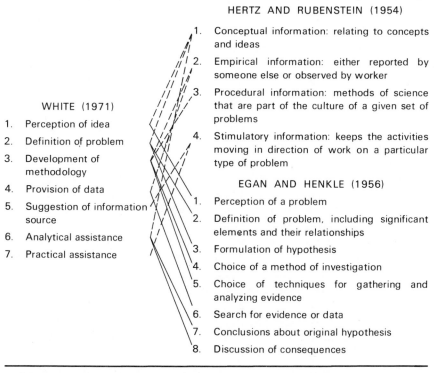

HERTZ AND RUBENSTEIN (1954)

1. Conceptual information: relating to concepts and ideas

2. Empirical information: either reported by someone else or observed by worker

3. Procedural information: methods of science that are part of the culture of a given set of problems

WHITE (1971)

1. Perception of idea

2. Definition of problem

3. Development of methodology

4. Provision of data

5. Suggestion of information source

6. Analytical assistance

7. Practical assistance

4. Stimulatory information: keeps the activities moving in direction of work on a particular type of problem

EGAN AND HENKLE (1956)

1. Perception of a problem

2. Definition of problem, including significant elements and their relationships

3. Formulation of hypothesis

4. Choice of a method of investigation

5. Choice of techniques for gathering and analyzing evidence

6. Search for evidence or data

7. Conclusions about original hypothesis

8. Discussion of consequences

[a] From White (1971) by permission of the author.

personal communication in science may occur among scientists in the same institution or among scientists in different institutions, among scientists in the same subject field or among scientists in different fields. It is now well established that there exists, in any scientific community, a personal network of professionals, related through similar research interests, institutional ties, or former associations, who maintain a close association by informing each other of ongoing and planned research, asking for criticism of draft papers or reports, discussing current work in correspondence or at conferences, and possibly collaborating on various joint projects. The "invisible college," as described, for example, by Crane (1972), is a personal network that tends to comprise an elite, influential, and cohesive group of workers engaged in research at the forefront of

their field. The invisible colleges are extremely effective information networks, but participation is largely restricted to those who are leaders in a
field, and it takes time for the younger, less experienced scientist to be
accepted into the appropriate network. The most structured and easily
recognized invisible colleges were those deliberately established by the
National Institutes of Health in its Information Exchange Group experiment of 1961–1967. The NIH in its Information Exchange Groups also
made a deliberate attempt to widen the network, bringing in the younger
scientists as well as scientists from countries less well developed than
those in the West. (See Cooper, 1968; Green, 1967; Heenan and
Weeks, 1971.)

A number of interesting sociometric analyses have been conducted in
the last few years. An excellent "model" is Crawford's investigation of
informal communication among scientists in the field of sleep research.
The techniques used by Crawford (1971) could be applied to any field of
research in order to determine the extent to which scientists in the field
communicate with each other and the extent to which they communicate with other professionals in outside fields. When the data from such
a study are plotted as a sociogram, a distinct communications network
can usually be discerned. While some *isolates* will be present, many
members of the research community are likely to be integrated into a
discernible network of the type shown in Figure 6, which is a sociogram
derived from Crawford's study in the sleep research community.
Although it may not be entirely clear within the great detail of this diagram, a comparatively small number of scientists account for a very large
proportion of all the contacts received, whereas some scientists will not
be contacted at all. This situation is made clear for the sleep community
in Table 3. From this table it can be seen that 99 scientists (45% of the
total community surveyed) were not contacted by anyone, whereas 23
scientists (11% of the community surveyed) received 54% of all the
contacts. "Thirty-three scientists initiated or received contacts from six or
more scientists; on the average, they were in contact with five times as
many sleep scientists as others in their research area [p. 303]." Such
individuals, who are likely to exist in any research community, may be
termed *central scientists* or *sociometric stars*. Lines of communication
converge on these individuals and, because they are foci for a large
number of professional contacts, they are in a position to supply information to a large number of other scientists. The sociometric stars play a
key role in information exchange within the community and they are the
people who will be most influential in the diffusion of innovations. In the
sleep community, the central scientists are themselves closely integrated

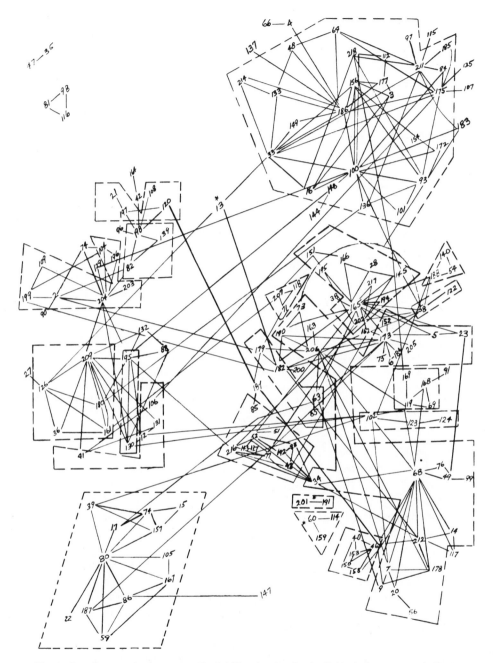

Figure 6. Communication network of 160 scientists in the field of sleep research. Each scientist is numbered; solid lines indicate communication between scientists; broken lines enclose scientists who work in the same research center. (From Crawford, 1971 by permission of John Wiley & Sons, Inc.)

TABLE 3

Number of Colleagues in Sleep Research Contacted by Sleep Scientists Three Times or More During the Past Year Concerning Their Work[a,b,c]

Contacts made		Contacts received	
Number of colleagues contacted by scientists	Distribution of scientists contacting	Number of scientists contacting colleagues	Distribution of colleagues contacted
0	71	0	99
1	42	1	38
2	35	2	32
3	26	3	13
4	18	4	9
5	13	5	4
6	4	6	7
7	4	7	1
8	3	8	3
9	2	9	3
10	—	10	3
11	—	≥ 11	6

[a] From Crawford (1971) by permission of John Wiley & Sons, Inc.

[b] Contacts made or received: $\bar{x} = 1.9$.

[c] The number of colleagues from whom contacts were received as well as the number of colleagues contacted are tabulated.

(Figure 7). All the stars are in direct contact with at least one other central scientist, with the exception of two who are one step removed.

Sociometric data, of the type illustrated, have great potential value in the planning of new information services and in the improvement of existing modes of communication within a research community. A sociogram shows how information spreads through a population. It reveals the routes by which information travels and it shows the way in which members are connected. Through a sociometric analysis it is possible to determine which investigators in a field communicate with each other so that information may be transferred among them. Crawford points out that it is possible to study the indirect communication of information $(i \rightarrow k \rightarrow j)$ as well as the direct communication $(i \rightarrow j)$, and to identify situations in which a message, if it reaches a particular scientist, is likely to go no farther. The analysis of sociometric data may reveal groups of scientists that have special importance in informal communication, groups in which members communicate intensively among themselves.

Crawford discovered that 218 scientists in the field of sleep research divided into a large network of 160 members, one group of two scientists, another group of three scientists, and 53 isolates who appear to communicate with no one (Figure 6). In the sleep community, 73% of all scientists seem to be connected, directly or indirectly, in a large informal communication network. The significance of a network of this kind cannot be overemphasized. In a rapidly changing field, a scientist

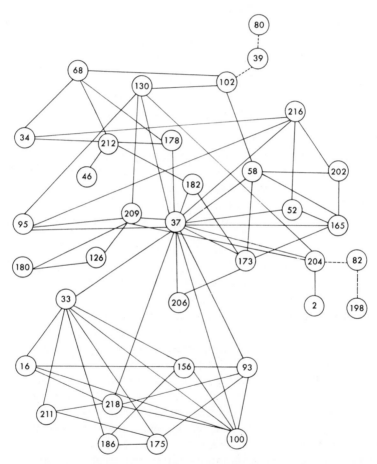

Figure 7. Map of communication relations between sociometrically central scientists (SCS). All SCS are in direct contact with at least one other SCS, with the exception of two scientists (80 and 198) who are in contact through a noncentral scientist. Broken lines indicate a contact through a noncentral scientist. (From Crawford, 1971 by permission of John Wiley & Sons, Inc.)

integrated within a communication network of this type is likely to receive information, and use it, much earlier than his nonintegrated colleagues. Coleman, Katz, and Menzel (1966), for example, were able to demonstrate the great value of a network of medical practitioners in the diffusion of drug information. A comparison of doctors integrated within the network with those not integrated led to the conclusion that the network had a very important effect on the early adoption of new drugs. DeGrolier (1975, p. 7-3) quotes Hamburger (1973) on the value of informal channels of communication, as follows:

> It is difficult . . . to recommend lists of books or articles to be read, as progress is so fast that written/i.e., printed/information is almost always obsolete when it is published; direct and constant contacts from researcher to researcher are the only way for following the advanced front. Here is a domain where telephone, jets, letters and unceasing small meetings on both sides of the Atlantic have become major research instruments.

It is very likely that those scientists who are most integrated within a network of informal communication will also be those who are most productive and most influential. As an example, Crawford found that the large network existing in the sleep community "contained all the scientists who are cited the most, read the most, contacted the most, and who produced the most papers |p. 305|." The isolates tend to be the less active participants in the research area.

A major purpose of a sociometric analysis of a scientific community is the identification of points of entry through which information can most effectively disseminate throughout a network. Crawford's analysis of the sleep research community identified a core of 33 scientists who are most contacted, most read, most cited, and most productive. The other research workers in the field are organized around these central scientists. They are located in the same laboratories, work with or under them (or have done so in the past), and go to them for advice and information. The sociometric stars are nodal points for the dissemination of information. Information transmitted to the 33 central scientists in sleep research could be transmitted to 95% of the scientists in the network through one intermediary scientist or less. The central scientists also appear to be highly influential in a number of ways; they can monitor and filter incoming information and, in all probability, can exert some control over what research is proposed and funded.

A special type of sociometric star has been identified by Allen (1975) as an "information gatekeeper" or "technological gatekeeper." Allen and other investigators have shown that engineers and scientists in a wide variety of industrial, governmental, and university settings rely very heavily on a small number of key people in their own organizations for the importation of information. These gatekeepers differ from their colleagues in being more oriented toward formal and informal sources of information outside their own organizations. They read more and maintain more extensive contacts with other individuals outside the organization. The gatekeeper is the star to whom many other individuals will turn when the need for information arises, and it is the gatekeeper who provides the most effective mechanism for bringing information into an organization. Allen, Piepmeier, and Cooney (1971) have also shown the existence of international technological gatekeepers, scientists who play a key role in the transfer of technology from one country to another.

The informal channels of communication, of course, are not restricted to the dissemination of oral information. They are also used to transmit various kinds of documents. In particular, authors tend to distribute multiple copies of reprints of their papers to other scientists either on demand or on an unsolicited basis. A survey of science authors undertaken by King *et al.* (1976) revealed that the average number of reprints obtained by authors was 128 in 1968 and that this had risen to 142 in 1975. By extrapolating to the universe of authors in science journals in the United States, it is possible to estimate that many millions of reprints are requested by science authors in this country alone, and that this volume is steadily rising. Since about 60% of these reprints are subsequently distributed, it is clear that reprint distribution plays a significant role in the complete picture of scientific communication.

There is one further finding on the information-seeking behavior of professionals that must be given careful consideration in the design of information services in any field. This finding relates to the importance of physical proximity and ease of use factors in the selection of information sources. Allen and Gerstberger (1967) produced evidence to show that, in selecting among a number of possible information sources, the source that is most convenient and easy to use is likely to be the one chosen, even when a less convenient source is perceived to be "better" (e.g., more complete, reliable, or up to date). These findings were substantiated by Rosenberg (1966). Ease of use, then, is probably the single most important factor determining whether or not a particular information service will be adopted by a community, a fact that was well recognized by Mooers (1960) and encapsulated in the now famous Mooers' Law: "An information retrieval system will tend *not* to be used when it is more painful and troublesome for a customer to have information than for him not to have it [p. ii].

It is the ease of use factor, as suggested in Chapter 3, that makes personal files so important as information sources. Personal files are important in the science field as well as the intelligence field, but their use has not been very extensively studied. Soper (1972), however, discovered that there is a strong tendency for a bibliographic item cited by an author to appear in his personal collection, and that this tendency applies to the humanities and socal sciences as well as to the field of science. It seems reasonable to suppose that, because of accessibility and ease of use factors, personal files are likely to be the first source to which many scientists will turn for certain kinds of information. If the personal files do not provide the information needed, the scientist is quite likely to turn next to an informal channel of communication, again because of ease of use factors. Formal information centers, including libraries, are likely to be further down the scale when information sources are ranked by priority of use.

This chapter has attempted to present a general overview of communication processes, formal and informal, in science and technology. It is not intended to be a complete and detailed account of this important subject, but it should at least highlight some characteristics of the present system that provide a needed background to the discussion of scientific and technical communication in a largely electronic world.

5

Some Problems of
Formal Communication in
Science and Technology

This chapter summarizes some of the problems faced by the scientist in the use of scientific literature, with special reference to its use for current awareness purposes. From the point of view of the individual scientist, four major problems can be identified:

1. The sheer volume of material that is submitted for publication and the rate at which this volume is increasing annually
2. Increasing fragmentation and specialization in science which tends to cause greater dispersion of the literature in which any one individual would be interested
3. The cost of publication
4. Delays in disseminating research information through formal communication channels

Each of these problems will be examined in turn. It should be noted that these problems are related to the packaging of the reports of scientific investigation for dissemination to the science community. In many ways these reports are not packaged very efficiently, for dissemination purposes, in the present system.

Growth of the Literature

As science itself grows in extension and intension and the number of active scientists increases, so obviously does the volume of literature generated by the scientific community. The growth of the literature itself has caused fairly widespread alarm and has been referred to in somewhat dramatic terms as the "literature explosion," the "information explosion," the "publication inflation," or the "publication pollution." Price (1963) claimed that the science literature has grown exponentially for the last three centuries, with a doubling rate of approximately 15 years[1], and Anderla (1973) presented some data to show that there is as yet no evidence that the limits to growth of this particular exponential phenomenon have been reached.

Let us look at some actual figures. The best indicator of the growth of the periodical literature of science and technology is very probably one derived from the growth of the National Lending Library for Science and Technology (now the British Library Lending Division) because this library has the most complete collection of periodicals in the field. As reported by Barr (1967), this library identified 26,235 periodical titles in science and technology in 1965 (22,619 already received and 3616 on order but not yet received), and this figure is the best estimate available for the size of the world population of scientific and technical journals a decade ago. The main justification for this figure is the fact that the library attempts to collect all periodicals that might contain materials of interest to the practicing scientist or technologist. No attempt is made to reject material on the basis of quality. Every unsatisfied request, from a worldwide population of users, is investigated and, when the title can be verified to exist, it is ordered and added to the collection. By 1974 the figure for titles received or on order was 49,440. Unfortunately, it is not possible to accept these figures, as they stand, as representing the actual rate of growth of the available periodical titles in science and technology because, in 1966, the library began to expand its scope beyond science and technology. If we make some reasonable allowances for this factor, however, and also for the fact that a journal acquired in a particular year may not have been first published in that year, it is possible to estimate that the world population of periodicals in science and technology is increasing at a rate of about 4% annually, and that in 1977 there were approximately 50,000 journals published worldwide in science and technology. It is important to recognize, however, that the literature

---

[1] De Grolier (1975), however, has suggested that these figures may be much exaggerated.

contains some wide discrepancies in estimates of the rate of growth of periodical titles. King *et al.* (1976) have reported estimates varying from as little as 2% a year to as great as 10%. For the growth of *scholarly* journals in science and technology, published in the United States, King *et al.* estimate an increase of 45% from 1960 to 1974, an average of 2.6% per year over the entire period. This figure is quite close to the estimate of the growth of scholarly journals in all fields in the United States, as reported by Fry and White (1975).

The growth in the number of periodical *titles* published is only one dimension of this problem, however. More significant is the increase in the total number of papers published. That is, the size of the information packages, as well as the number of these packages, is important. Not only is the number of journals increasing, but the majority of journals are also increasing in size each year as more papers are submitted and accepted for publication. A study conducted by the National Academy of Sciences–National Academy of Engineering (1970), based on a sample of 50 journals, reported a median growth rate of about 7% a year over about a 10-year period, although wide variations from journal to journal were observed (from zero growth to about 14% growth). The NAS–NAE report indicates that some major journals have been growing at a rate greater than the total growth of their respective fields. The *Physical Review*, for example, grew from 1.97 megawords in 1937 to 22 megawords in 1968, which represents a doubling rate of about 7 or 8 years. In the same time period, the *Journal of Chemical Physics* grew from .82 megawords to 10.4 megawords. Some journals are growing even faster than this. Sandoval *et al.* (1976) report that *Biochimica et Biophysica Acta* has been growing at an approximately logarithmic rate since its foundation in 1947. This journal now doubles in size approximately every 4.6 years.

Narin and Carpenter (1974) presented growth rate, in number of articles published, for a sample of 492 large or heavily cited journals in seven major scientific disciplines. These data indicate a growth of 33.6% in a 7-year period for physics and geophysics journals, and a rate of growth of 31% in the same period for chemistry and metallurgy journals. Averaged over the 7 years, this represents an annual growth rate of between 4% and 4.2%. A report issued by the National Science Foundation (1964), based on a sample of 262 scientific journals, reports a 52% increase in a decade, which also works out to an average annual growth of about 4.3%. Metzner (1973) has reported that the number of pages printed by the American Institute of Physics doubles about every 8 years and has done so back to 1940.

Finally, King *et al.* (1976) calculated the total number of articles published in scholarly journals in science and technology in the United States to be 105,932 in 1960 and 155,345 in 1975. The rate of increase is calculated to be 14% for the period of 1960–1965, 17% for 1965–1970, and 10% for 1970–1975.

For our present purposes, it is not important to know in absolute terms what the rate of growth figure is. In any case, we will get variations by subject field and by time period. In some fields, for some periods, the rate of publication will actually decline. The Narin and Carpenter (1974) data, for example, indicate that the number of papers published in engineering and mathematics increased for some years until 1971 but declined in 1972. The important thing to recognize is that the product of the growth in periodical titles published and the growth in the size of these periodicals represents a very substantial annual increase in the amount of published literature available in all scientific and technical fields. But, while this literature grows exponentially, the time that any one scientist has for reading this literature remains more or less the same from year to year. Clearly, then, the scientist is faced with two possibilities:

1.   He can resign himself to the fact that, if he spends time in the direct scanning of the literature, he will be able to cover less and less of the total of literature of potential relevance to his interests, or

2.   He must use more efficient procedures for finding those items, from the total published, that are most likely to be of interest.

As the literature grows, and the sources multiply, it becomes more difficult to undertake comprehensive retrospective searches, as well as to survey the literature for current awareness purposes.

Although the journal is regarded as the major primary publication in science, there are other forms with which the scientist must concern himself, and all of these are growing. In the United States there were 5203 new books (hardcover) or new editions published in science and technology in 1965. The comparable figure for 1974 was 7314, an increase of more than 40% in less than 10 years. In addition, volumes of conference proceedings now seem to be published at the rate of about 7000 items a year, with over 2000 of these in the science and technology area.

A good indicator of the growth of the technical report literature is the number of reports indexed and/or abstracted by the National Technical Information Service (NTIS) and the Defense Documentation Center (DDC), these organizations being the major disseminators in the United States of the unclassified and the classified report literature, respectively.

According to figures released by the National Federation of Abstracting and Indexing Services, these two agencies processed 77,742 items in 1965 and 90,496 items in 1973. This represents a rate of increase of 16.4% in 8 years.

In the period 1960–1974, the number of patents issued in the United States increased from 50,000 to 80,000. That is, in 1974 the number issued was about 60% greater than the number issued in 1960. In 1965 there were 8865 new dissertations listed for the science field in *Dissertation Abstracts International* (U.S. and Canadian universities), but in 1974 the corresponding figure was 15,606.

No good figures exist for the growth of translations in science and technology. Perhaps the best indicator, however, is the growth of the National Translations Center (the John Crerar Library, Chicago) whose collections numbered 107,620 items in 1965 and had more than doubled to 216,238 items by 1974. Although the NTC is not completely restricted to science and technology, the great majority of the translations do fall in this area. The very least we can say about these data is that they represent the rate of growth of the body of foreign technical literature, translated into English, that is most accessible and best controlled.

Bernal (1959) succinctly pinpointed the problems caused simply by the growth of the literature as follows: "The amount to be read increases exponentially, and the time anyone has for reading it remains the same; therefore a smaller proportion of what is written is read by any one person [p. 80]." This fact lends credibility to the assertion, sometimes made, that the author of a scientific document now has less chance of having his work read, understood, and applied than at any previous period in the history of science.

While it is an undeniable fact that the literature of science is growing at an exponential rate, not everyone agrees that this rate of growth is really serious in itself. It has been suggested by several writers that as the literature has grown, its overall quality has declined, and that the volume of really significant and original contributions to this literature is certainly not growing exponentially. Mellanby (1967), for example, estimated that the number of pages used to communicate the new results of original research in Britain only doubled in the period of 1936–1966.

Bar-Hillel (1963) has also claimed that the information explosion has been exaggerated; at least, he maintains, the growth of the literature has not in itself created a crisis in scientific communication, as many others have contended. Bar-Hillel points out that the growth of the literature is "commensurate with the increase in scientific and technological manpower and is, in fact, nothing more than its direct result [p. 98]."

Moreover, he claims, a scientist does not need to allocate more time each year to keeping up with the literature because he himself will become increasingly specialized in his interests. The increase in his specialization will tend, therefore, to compensate for the growth of the literature.

If we accept the claim that the volume of the really significant scientific literature is growing at a much slower rate than the volume of the total scientific literature, this should be a cause for sorrow rather than rejoicing because it tends only to exacerbate the problems. It means, in fact, that the literature of science is becoming more dilute. It is also likely that the really significant papers in a field will be scattered throughout a larger number of journals, making it increasingly difficult for the scientist to find them. The comparatively small number of journals that the scientist can scan on a regular basis will contain a smaller and smaller proportion of the total literature published in his or her field of specialization. At the same time, the direct relevance of the overall contents of any journals to which the scientist subscribes (or regularly scans through other sources) is quite likely to be diminishing. That is, for any one reader, the proportion of the papers published annually in any journal that is directly relevant to his or her interests is likely to decline over the years. As a result, it becomes more and more difficult for the reader to separate the wheat from the chaff. Furthermore, because subscription rates are increasing, the cost to the scientist for each relevant paper found is likely to be growing at a rapid rate.

Several writers, including Price (1964), have criticized the motives for publication. The "publish or perish" phenomenon, tied to promotion and career development, encourages quantity of publication, possibly at the expense of quality. Price urges self-restraint on the part of scientists. In particular, scientists must avoid multiple publication of essentially the same research results. Others have strongly recommended more stringent refereeing procedures as a means of screening out the less noteworthy contributions to the literature. Brown, Pierce, and Traub (1967), however, are strongly critical of this. They point out that the growth of science inevitably causes a decline in the proportion of outstanding papers published because the total number of scientists increases more or less as the square of the number of outstanding ones. The growth of science, then, inevitably leads to an increase in the amount of literature published. To restrict deliberately the volume of publication would be to deny the growth of science itself.

So far we have spoken only of the growth of the primary literature. The secondary literature must inevitably be growing at about the same rate. According to De Grolier (1975), the first published abstracts of the

periodical literature began to appear in 1715, and now the world population of indexing and abstracting services (Ashworth, 1974) is estimated
to be about 3500, with some 1500 of these in science and technology.
The increasing application of the computer in the production of secondary services, as mentioned in Chapter 2, has greatly increased the ease
with which specialized bibliographies and indexes can be produced on a
regular basis, so the growth rate of such secondary services is likely to
be particularly great for the period since 1965 and to continue at a high
rate for some time to come.

Of course, the secondary services are growing in size as well as
number in an attempt to keep up with the growth of the primary litera-
ture. For example, the number of items processed annually by the
members of the National Federation of Abstracting and Indexing
Services, which represents most of the major secondary services in the
United States, increased from 884,000 in 1965 to 1,590,000 in 1975.
A more dramatic demonstration of this phenomenon is provided by
Ashworth (1974), who points out that it took the Chemical Abstracts
Service about 32 years (1907–1938) to publish its first million abstracts,
18 years to publish the second million, 8 years for the third, 4.75 years
for the fourth, and only 3.3 years for the fifth. It is clear that, if this rate
continues, the service must soon include a million abstracts a year if it is
to get anywhere close to a comprehensive coverage of the literature of
chemistry.

Literature Scatter

The quantity and quality of papers produced create problems for the
publisher of science materials as well as for the user of science publications. There are two other closely related problems that affect both the
publisher and the user of science literature:

1. Increasing specialization in science
2. The fragmentation or dispersion of the literature on a particular
    subject

Individual scientists or research teams tend to focus on increasingly narrow areas of study. This increasing specialization creates problems in the
efficient "packaging" of science papers. The more scientists specialize,
and the greater the volume of literature published, the less efficient
become the major journals that attempt to cover a broad area of science.
A journal of broad scope in, say, physics is likely to be less and less successful in meeting the needs of the scientist for the simple reason that

proportionately fewer papers, over the years, will be of direct interest to any one individual. Elsdon-Dew (1955), for example, estimated that any particular article in a highly specialized periodical is likely to be of interest to only about 10% of the workers in the subject area covered, an article in a general periodical may be of interest to only 2% of the readers, and an article in a local publication may be of interest to as few as one-quarter of 1% of the scientists in the field. Certain other studies of the readership of journals have revealed that, while a few papers may be quite widely read, many are read by very few scientists, and some are apparently not read at all. Sorokin (1968) mentions a measurement of this phenomenon, named the *Makulatorfactor*, which is defined as:

$$m = \frac{S - S'}{S} \times 100$$

where

S = the number of pages in the journal
S' = the number of pages read by the user (determined by questionnaire)

Wass, the originator of the formula, is said to have estimated the *Makulatorfactor* for the scientific literature of 1960 and arrived at a factor of 85%. The implication is that millions of journal pages published remain unread.

Some interesting figures on the extent of "current" readership were derived by the American Psychological Association (1963) for journals published by that society. Based on an extensive study, it was determined that about one-half of the research reports in "core" psychology journals were read or scanned, within 2 months of publication, by 1% or less of a random sample of psychologists. At the highest end of the current readership distribution, no research report is likely to be read by more than about 7% of such a sample. Even the most popular journals (seen by 20% of the sample) contained a sizable percentage of articles that were examined by less than 1% of the sample in the time period under review. Thus, the immediate audience for most articles is obviously of an extremely restricted size.

Moore (1972) reported on a readership survey of the *Journal of Organic Chemistry*. The average subscriber glanced at or began to read about 17% of the papers in a typical issue, and read half or more of only 4% of the papers in the issue. The average time spent in reading a 413-page journal was only 2.2 hours.

With journal publication in its present form, it is quite possible that an individual subscriber may have to pay for 20 or 30 papers that do not directly concern him in order to get one paper of direct relevance. This situation has led to an increase in the number of highly specialized journals, and it has forced some of the broader journals to split into more specialized sections to avoid a heavy loss of authors and readers to the younger journals of narrower scope.

This increasing fragmentation in science publishing contributes to the increasing scatter or dispersion of the literature of a particular subject. The phenomenon of the dispersion of the literature of a particular subject throughout many sources was reported by Bradford (1948). Bradford discovered that, if a comprehensive literature search is undertaken on some subject, for a particular time period, the collection of articles discovered is likely to be drawn from a very large number of journals. He also discovered, however, that a comparatively small number of "key" journals contribute a very large number of all the articles in a particular subject field. If all the sources (journals) contributing papers are ranked in order of decreasing productivity (yield) of papers, the ranked list can be divided into zones, each succeeding zone containing journals of decreasing productivity. If the division into zones is done in such a way that each contributes an approximately equal number of articles on the subject, the relationship from zone to zone will be roughly geometric according to the series:

$$I : n : n^2 \cdots n^{10}$$

where I represents the number of journals in the first zone ("nucleus") and n is a multiplier. To take a simple example, it might be found that 155 separate journals contribute 375 papers on a particular subject in a 5-year period. Suppose we divide the ranked list of journals so that we have three zones of journals, each zone contributing 125 articles. The first zone might be found to contain only 5 high productivity journals, the second 25 (i.e., 5×5), and the third 125 (5×5^2). In the third zone, each journal contributes only one paper to the subject.

This distribution of papers over sources, which has since been shown to hold in all subject fields when a comprehensive search is undertaken, is frequently referred to as the *Bradford distribution* and the phenomenon as Bradford's *law of scattering*. For any subject field, for any time period, if we plot the cumulative percentage of articles published against the cumulative percentage of journals contributing (sources), we will get a curve of the general type shown in Figure 8. There are several other

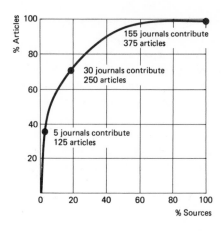

Figure 8. Dispersion of the journal literature in a particular subject field.

ways of plotting this distribution, some more mathematically exact, but
this figure gives the general picture quite well. The distribution closely
resembles the distribution of the use of words in written text as observed
by Zipf (1949).

In this example (Figure 8), it takes 155 journals to achieve 100%
coverage of the journal literature, but 66% coverage is achieved by as
few as 30 journals, and 33% coverage by only 5. This dispersion is
important because it illustrates clearly the futility of trying to keep up to
date in a scientific field solely by scanning the primary literature. In the
hypothetical situation illustrated in Figure 8, a scientist who regularly
scans 5 journals has the possibility of finding 33% of the journal literature
in his subject field, but only if he is fortunate enough to select the 5
journals of highest yield. If he scans as many as 30 journals regularly (a
somewhat unlikely situation), he has the possibility of finding 66% of the
literature, but only if he chooses the top 30 titles on the ranked list (even
less likely). One thing is quite certain: He will not get close to 100%
coverage by direct scanning of the literature. The problem, as stated
earlier, is largely one of efficient packaging. The science journal is not an
efficient way of packaging the results of science research for dissemination purposes—the papers of potential interest to a particular scientist
are likely to be dispersed over many packages, and the packages he is
able to scan regularly are likely to contain a high proportion of items that
are of no direct interest to him.

The situation illustrated in Figure 8, while hypothetical, is quite
typical. Leith (1969), for example, found that the distribution of sources
represented in his personal collection of reprints (in radiation and cell
biology) was Bradfordian. He suggested that a scientist might be able to

cover about 55% of the literature of potential relevance to him by the direct scanning of a small number of key journals.

In Figure 9 we have elaborated on Figure 8 in order to depict what may be a typical current awareness situation in the sciences. A scientist who scans a number of key journals in his field (the exact number will vary from field to field, perhaps as few as 6 or as many as 20) might cover 50 to 60% of the journal literature that matches his current professional interests. To get a substantially better coverage he would need to scan secondary services or, better yet, receive SDI service from the machine-readable data bases of these services. Depending on the subject field, he may need to use more than one secondary service or data base to push his coverage up to, say, 90%. Even through secondary services, however, he is unlikely to go much beyond a 90% figure in current awareness activities. Nevertheless, SDI service from secondary data bases is a much more cost-effective approach to current awareness than subscribing to journals. In the chemistry and physics area, for example, a scientist might buy SDI service for, say, $200 a year and this service might yield references to 80% of the literature of relevance to his current research interests. At 1976 prices, $200 would buy only 4 journals in these fields on the average, and these 4 journals, even if chosen optimally, are unlikely to yield more than 25% of the relevant literature.

It is important to note, however, that the degree of dispersion of the literature will vary from one subject field to another. In fact, it seems reasonable to suppose, as Brookes (1973) and Buckland (1972) have suggested, that the age of a subject field, its scatter, and its rate of obsolescence are all related. The rate at which the literature of this field is growing (i.e., its doubling rate) also fits into this picture. Thus, when a

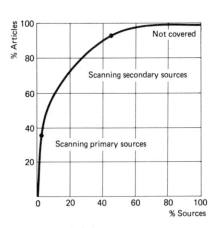

Figure 9. Typical current awareness problem faced by a scientist.

new field of study develops (say, the field of laser technology), the literature is very compact, is doubling in a matter of months, and is obsoles-
cing rather rapidly. As the field develops, over the years, the literature
will become more dispersed, and the rates of both growth and obsolescence will decline.

The situation depicted in Figure 9 is, of course, oversimplified in a
number of respects. For one thing, it assumes that current awareness
activities are all based on published information sources, whereas we
know that informal channels of communication will be of at least equal
importance to many scientists. But, as pointed out earlier, it takes time
for a scientist to become well integrated into a particular research community, and the degree of his integration is likely to be related to the
country in which he lives and the institutions at which he has worked or
studied.

It could also be argued that Figure 9 presents an unnecessarily
gloomy picture in that it implies that all articles have equal value. It is
possible that the majority of the really important articles in any field will
appear in the core journals and that the articles appearing in the journals
within the long tail of the distribution will be those of lesser importance.
This theory, while attractive, has never been proven and, in fact, is
somewhat unlikely. The "long tail of the distribution" does not reflect any
qualitative differences among journals but merely the probability that a
particular journal will include articles on a particular subject. A major
medical journal may contribute only one article in 10 years that is
directly relevant to the copper industry, but that article, exposing previously unknown hazards, may have greater impact on the industry than
all the articles published in metals journals in the course of a year. Yet it
is precisely this type of article that is difficult to find by conventional
approaches to current awareness because, not only is the journal unlikely
to be scanned regularly by the copper industry, but it is also unlikely to
be covered by the secondary services that the industry will regularly use.

The fact is that Figure 9 gives an optimistic picture of the current
awareness problem rather than a pessimistic one because it depicts only
one facet of the problem, namely, current awareness of relevant articles
published in science journals. Depending on the precise subject field, the
practitioner in science and technology is unlikely to be truly well
informed unless he also keeps up to date with new developments
reflected in other types of literature, including books, reports, conference
papers, patents, dissertations, translations, and, possibly, standards and
specifications. Not only is the practitioner unable to keep up with the
range of new literature by direct scanning, but he must also use a
number of secondary sources to keep current because no one source will
give close to a complete coverage.

Cost of the Literature

It is unfortunate for the process of scientific communication that the costs of at least some types of publications, over the last several years, have been increasing at a very fast rate and far in excess of the increase in more general indicators of inflation rate. One of the problems is that the publishing industry is still very labor-intensive. Because it has not yet benefited appreciably from automation activities, it lags behind many other industries in terms of improved productivity. The Industrial Production Index for all U.S. industry went up from 100 to 124.8 between 1967 and 1974, but the increase in the printing and publishing industry was from 100 to 112.3 only, while the rubber and plastics industry rose from 100 to 164.4 in this period. Data presented by King *et al.* (1976) on the costs of journal publishing indicate that it is labor costs that are largely responsible for the price increases. They show, for example, that the average hourly wage of a union printer more than doubled ($3.85 to $7.95) from 1966 to 1976, and that the average rate for a managing editor increased more than 70% in the same period. Postal rates too have a significant impact on the costs of publishing. King *et al.* (1976) show that these rates increased by over 100% from 1962 to 1974 and are expected to increase by an additional 110% by 1980.

Increases in materials costs are also of significance. Senders *et al.* (1975) point out that paper costs amount to about 30% of the total costs of printing a journal and that, while the cost of paper increased linearly from 1940 to 1970, very considerable increases have occurred since that time. Under the best of conditions, they estimate that paper costs may double again in the period 1975–1980; under the worst of conditions, they may treble. One publisher alone, the American Psychological Association, spent about $300,000 on paper in 1973 and $400,000 in 1975. According to Senders *et al.* (1975), APA may be spending $800,000 or more in 1980, but only if the amount they publish remains more or less at present levels (an unlikely situation).

It can be argued, of course, that subscriber income is also increasing and that increased subscriber income will offset inflation in publishing costs. The validity of this argument can be tested by examining publication costs in constant dollars as well as current dollars. "Current dollars" refers to the actual amount paid for a publication whereas "constant dollars" are derived by applying an implicit "Gross National Product deflator" in order to relate the purchasing power of a dollar to its purchasing power in a base year. King *et al.* (1976) use 1967 as the base year for their cost figures, and Table 4 presents some of their data from 1960 to 1975 for various categories of publication.

In terms of current dollars, the increases are all very considerable,

TABLE 4

Average Cost of Various Types of Publication, 1960–1975

Publication	1960	1965	1966	1967	1970	1975
Hardcover book[a] in science and technology						
Current dollars	7.74	10.08	10.34	10.29	13.33	16.63
Constant dollars	8.81	10.69	10.67	10.29	11.59	10.64
Hardcover book[a] in medicine						
Current dollars	8.41	11.88	12.37	12.78	18.05	18.91
Constant dollars	9.57	12.60	12.77	12.78	15.69	11.96
Scholarly journal[a]						
Current dollars	7.88	14.42	15.07	16.48	21.78	29.18
Constant dollars	8.97	15.29	15.55	16.48	18.94	18.45
Journal in chemistry and physics[b]						
Current dollars	11.30	18.42	19.73	22.35	33.45	65.57
Technical reports in paper copy[c]						
Current dollars			1.55	2.38	3.15	5.07
Constant dollars			1.60	2.38	2.74	3.21
Technical reports in microform[c]						
Current dollars			0.35	0.49	0.38	0.60
Constant dollars			0.38	0.49	0.33	0.38

[a] From King et al. (1976).

[b] From the Bowker Annual of Library and Book Trade Information.

[c] These figures, from King et al. (1976), are derived by dividing total sales volume for the National Technical Information Service by total sales income.

with quite dramatic increases for certain categories of material. The average cost of a book in medicine, for example, went from $12.37 in 1966 to $18.91 in 1975. In the same period, the average price of a technical report in paper copy more than doubled, and the average price of a subscription to a journal in chemistry or physics went from $19.73 to $65.57, an increase of well over 200% in less than 10 years. Some journals, of course, have recorded price increases substantially above these averages. De Gennaro (1977) indicates that *Inorganica Chimica Acta* raised its price to libraries from $26 in 1970 to $235 in 1975, a staggering jump of 804%. King et al. (1976) project an annual cost of $123.37 for a journal in chemistry and physics by 1980, and an average cost of a technical report in paper copy to be $6.80 by 1980. They report an increase of 232% in the cost of a technical report from 1966 to 1974, if bought in paper copy, and an increase in cost of 97% if bought in microfiche form. Increases in "subscriber income" are not even close to many of these cost increases.

Even considered as constant dollars, many of the price increases have been considerable when taken over various 5-year periods. King *et al.* (1976) show, for example, that the average increase in the cost of a medical book was 32% in constant dollars (41% in current dollars) from 1960 to 1965, and 25% in constant dollars (52% in current dollars) from 1965 to 1970. In the period 1970–1975, the average cost of technical report in paper copy increased 18% in constant dollars and 61% in current dollars, while costs for microform copies went up 20% in constant dollars and 60% in current dollars for this period. From 1965 to 1970, the average individual subscription price to a scholarly journal went up 20% in constant dollars and over 100% in current dollars.

It is in the costs of secondary publication, however, that increases have been most dramatic. King *et al.* (1976) report an increase in the average cost per item processed by the secondary services from $23.20 to $37.40 in the period 1965–1974. The following figures (King *et al.*, 1976) are examples of subscription increases for some major abstracting or indexing services in science and technology:

	1963	1968	1973	Percentage increase 1963–1973
Bibliography of Agriculture	$10	$19	$95	850%
Biological Abstracts	$225	$600	$1000	340%
Chemical Abstracts	$1000	$1550	$2400[a]	140%
Index Medicus	$40	$72	$155	290%
Psychological Abstracts	$20	$30	$190	850%

[a] The 1976 price was $3500.

It should be noted that none of these services is produced by a truly commercial organization. Three are produced by societies or noncommercial organizations and two by agencies of the government. Nor are such dramatic price increases limited to the major services or to services originating in the United States. If we wish to cast back further in time, the increases are even more dramatic in some respects. It is hard to believe, for example, that it was possible for a chemist to subscribe to Chemical Abstracts for $12 a year in 1940, and less than this if he was a member of the American Chemical Society. At $12 a year, *Chemical Abstracts* was within the means of many practicing chemists. At $3500 a year, it is now within the means of only the wealthier institutions.

What is quite clear from these figures is that, to keep up with literature growth plus increasing production costs, the major indexing and abstracting services have long since priced themselves out of the pocket of the individual subscriber, and have become a purely institutional (i.e., library) phenomenon. There is a danger that the same thing will happen to the science journal if it continues to be published in its present form. According to Baumol and Ordover (1976), "a growing proportion of scientific journals have virtually no individual subscribers, but are sold almost exclusively to libraries [p. 460]." De Gennaro (1977) claims that "many commercial publishers have lost interest in personal subscribers and no longer quote rates for them in their advertising copy [p. 71]." Fry and White (1975) produce data to show that the proportion of institutional to total subscribers for a large sample of scholarly journals increased from 56.1% to 56.9% in the case of commercial journals, in the period 1969–1973. For society journals the comparable increase is 22.6% to 25.5%, and for university press journals from 50.4% to 53.5%. Although these increases may not seem particularly dramatic, they do represent significant swings toward the institutional subscriber in a very short time period. Such changes appear inevitable. In fact, it seems reasonable to suppose that, if scientific publication continues in its present form, the primary journal subscriptions will continue to move to the institutional subscriber while the major secondary services will move increasingly out of the reach of the smaller or less wealthy libraries. The general accessibility of the literature declines as a result.

Publication Delays

King *et al.* (1976) present the best available data on the delays occurring from the time a paper is submitted for publication to the time it appears in a science journal. The average publishing lag for all fields of science was reported to be 9.4 months in 1974, but some fields showed much longer average delays. In computer science the delay was reported to be 17.8 months in 1974, and in mathematics and statistics it was 14.9 months. There is some evidence that the most consistent increases in publishing delays in the period of 1962–1974 are associated with those fields (physical sciences, environmental sciences, computer sciences) in which there have been the greatest percentage increases in the number of articles published, suggesting that increases in the amount written were "outstripping journal capacity" in these fields. There appears, however, to be some leveling off in the increase in publishing delays after 1970.

There are further delays, of course, from the time a journal article is published to the time it is indexed and/or abstracted in the secondary services. Some examples of these delays are given in the literature. Ashmole, Smith, and Stern (1973), for example, in evaluating various secondary data bases in terms of their timely coverage of pharmaceutical information, discovered that the *Science Citation Index* data base averaged delays in the range of zero to 3 weeks from time of publication, while most other services averaged 2–6 months, and *Biological Abstracts* averaged 4–12 months.

As science itself grows, the amount that is written increases and more is submitted for publication. This has a tendency to increase publication delays, in some cases by very considerable amounts. Because of the amount submitted, the costs of publication, and the need to keep journal growth within reasonable bounds, many publishers are forced to reject manuscripts because of accumulated publishing backlogs rather than on the basis of scientific merit. Some professional societies have reported that a substantial number of the papers now rejected are really worth publication and would be accepted if the societies could afford to publish more. Rejection of a worthwhile paper does not usually prevent publication, since it is likely to be submitted to other publishers, but it can cause considerable delays in publication. Shephard (1973) cites the case of an important medical paper that was submitted to five journals before it was eventually accepted. The resulting publication delay was one of 21 months. A more complete analysis of the effect of manuscript rejection on publication delays in the physical and social sciences is given by Garvey, Lin, and Nelson (1970). Roistacher (1978) has reported that the journal *Sociometry* received 550 manuscripts for review in 1974 but had space to publish only 39 articles. Burchinal (1975), quoting Machlup, refers to the present journal system as being in a "strangulation situation": "Manuscript pressure, a reflection of the increasing scientific and engineering work force, is rising, but journals cannot be expanded because of rising costs and decreased individual and institutional subscriptions [p. 174]."

It is convenient to consider publishing delays in science as part of a broader picture. In an efficient system for scientific communication, it is reasonable to expect that information on the existence of a research project should be disseminated throughout the science community at the earliest possible time. The science journal, although it may be considered to have important social and archival roles to play in science, is not a very efficient mechanism for the dissemination of information relating to current scientific research. A research project reported in a journal article will usually have been *completed* some months (and possibly over a year) earlier, and it could well have been *begun* some 3 years or more earlier. A current awareness device that tells us about projects begun 3 years past and concluded 1 year ago can hardly be regarded as very current. The secondary services, of course, are even less current. It is an unfortunate fact that most "current awareness" services of a formal nature are based on secondary data bases that are very far from being current. These data bases lag some months behind the science journal which, in turn, lags months or even years behind *current* research.

The situation can perhaps best be illustrated by considering a hypothetical research project and determining in what ways, and at what time, information on the *existence* of this project could conceivably reach the science community through various communication channels. This is done in Figure 10, which depicts (a) the history of a hypothetical research project, (b) the dissemination of information on or from this research project through informal channels of communication, (c) the dissemination of information on or from this research project through published primary sources, and (d) the dissemination of information on or from this research project through published secondary sources. The history and publication cycle is hypothetical. It represents, in fact, an optimum situation rather than a typical situation.

The hypothetical research project, of 24 months duration, is supported by a research grant from the federal government. The science community has the ability to learn of the existence of this project shortly before or shortly after its inception in one of two ways:

1.   Assuming that the investigators are well integrated into an invisible college structure (i.e., they are not isolates), information on the existence of the project will tend to spread very rapidly through the informal channels of communication provided by the invisible college. Crawford (1971), among others, has shown that information reaching the invisible college will tend to spread rapidly and contagiously, like an infection, throughout this community. Indeed, certain members of the invisible college, particularly the sociometric stars, may learn of the research project before it is actually underway. That is, they will know of its existence at the proposal stage, either because the research proposal has been submitted to one or more members of the community, by the investigators, in an informal way, or because leading members of the community have been asked to review it formally by the funding agency. Awareness of the research project by this means is, of course, limited to those scientists who are well integrated socially within the science community.

2.   If things go as they should, an abstract of the research proposal will get into the machine-readable data base of the Smithsonian Science Information Exchange (SSIE). This project description

should be accessible shortly after the grant is awarded (let us say 3 months after the beginning of the project). Unlike the informal channels of the invisible college, the services of SSIE are available to anyone who knows of their existence and is willing to use them. If a scientist learns of the existence of a project through SSIE, he or she has the ability to contact the investigators directly in order to obtain further information.

Theoretically at least, it might be possible to learn of the existence of this research project through primary sources after it has been in progress for 3 to 6 months. It may be a requirement of the funding agency that the investigators submit quarterly progress reports. If the research is not "classified" (in a security sense), these progress reports should be deposited with the National Technical Information Service (NTIS), and they would be announced in the various current awareness mechanisms of this agency. The classified report literature would also be announced by the appropriate agencies (e.g., the Defense Documentation Center). For those who use the report literature, then, the project could be accessible some 6 months or so after its inception, assuming optimum conditions.

Twelve months after the beginning of the project, a progress report might be presented to the community at large in the form of a conference paper. The project thus becomes accessible to those scientists who attend professional meetings and to those others who are sociometrically linked to these attendees. Conceivably, the conference organizers will require that the authors submit a copy of their paper in advance of the meeting and that printed conference proceedings be available at the time of the meeting. In other situations, preprints of the papers may be made and distributed. In many cases, however, no printed conference papers will be available, or they will appear, as proceedings, only many months after the conference.

The existence of forthcoming conferences can, of course, be learned from lists of future meetings, such lists appearing as separate publications or in certain scientific and technical journals. The specific topics of papers to be presented at a forthcoming meeting can be learned from the programs of these meetings, distributed in advance by the organizers. The topics of papers presented at scientific meetings can also be learned from the publication *Current Programs*, issued by Data Courier Inc., Lousiville, Kentucky. Such listings of conference papers, and indexes to them, should theoretically appear before the conferences to which they relate (i.e., they should serve as advance alerting devices). Regrettably, many papers are listed only after the conference has taken place. Nevertheless, a paper may be presented at a conference many months before a formal journal article appears. A scientist may learn of the existence of a research project through such lists of conference papers and may then contact the investigators directly. In some subject fields an organization may assume the responsibility of producing a synopsis of what occurred at a particular conference. The Brain Information Service at UCLA, for example, has produced synopses of this kind in various aspects of neurology. They would be available a few weeks after the conference has taken place.

In the hypothetical case of Figure 10, the first reference to the research project to appear in the scientific journal literature occurs, some 18 months after the inception of the project, as a brief communication or letter in a "letters" journal. At this point the project becomes accessible to those scientists who scan journals and to those who make use of *Current Contents*.[2] It is likely, in most cases, to be some months before this brief communication is indexed or abstracted in one of the major secondary services. Thus, those scientists who rely on the scanning of indexing or abstracting publications, or on SDI service based on a machine-readable data base derived from such publications, will only learn of the research project many months after its inception (approximately 2 years later in the hypothetical case of Figure 10), and possibly only after the project is ended. This assumes, also, the publication of a brief communication while the project is still proceeding. If such a brief communication is not prepared, it is quite likely that the first journal article (a full account of the project) will not appear until some months after the project is concluded. Under the best of circumstances, the article may appear 6 months after the termination of the project. More likely, however, it will not appear for a year or more. In this situation (i.e., no brief communication published), the project becomes accessible through scanning of the primary literature, or through *Current Contents*, some 36 months after the beginning of the project and some 12 months after its termination. Under these circumstances, the project is only likely to become accessible through the secondary literature (including machine-readable data bases derived from this literature)

---

[2] *Current Contents* is a publication of the Institute for Scientific Information (ISI). Published in sections corresponding to various branches of science, it reproduces the contents pages of current journals in the field. In Figure 10, *Current Contents* is shown to appear at approximately the same time as the journal issues to which it relates. It may, in fact, lag by a few weeks. Through special arrangements with journal publishers, whereby proofs of contents pages are delivered to ISI before actual publication, it is theoretically possible for a contents page to appear in *Current Contents* before the journal is published. This appears to be a rare occurrence.

between 3 and 4 years after the inception of the research. Note, however, that here we are referring to secondary publications, and services, based primarily on the journal literature. Secondary services that include conference literature, or the technical report literature, will be more current.

Some additional months are likely to elapse between the time the research project is first reported in a scientific journal and the time the project has been "assimilated" by the scientific community to the extent that it is first cited by other writers. In the case illustrated, the brief communication is cited some 9 months later (i.e., some 27 months after the project began). The first full journal article would be cited correspondingly later. Here, of course, we are making the assumption that the research project is sufficiently important to be cited by other writers. Allowing for some delay in the publication of the *Science Citation Index*,[3] it would be reasonable to assume that the project first becomes accessible through this source some 30 months or so after the research began. This, again, assumes an optimum situation, one in which a brief communication appears in the journal literature.

Maintaining this assumption further, it would be reasonable to suppose that the project might first be accessible through an annual review about 30 months after commencement of the project. Once more, a somewhat optimum situation is postulated, one in which an annual review is published and the review appears fairly rapidly. However, if the writer of the review article makes use of the report literature, or of conference preprints, he could conceivably bring this project to the attention of the science community at a somewhat earlier time.

Finally, it is possible that the results of the research project will be written up and published as a monograph; it is unlikely that such a volume will appear until some 24 months after the conclusion of the project (i.e., some 4 years or more after the research began).

The hypothetical data of Figure 10 give an indication of how rapidly various sources or media of communication will provide awareness of a research project of some importance to the science community. It should be clear from this diagram that, while some sources are truly current, others are useful mostly for archival or retrospective search purposes rather than for current awareness. The same data are presented in a somewhat different way in Table 5. This table is essentially a ranked list of sources in order of importance for purposes of current awareness. It

---

[3] Here we are assuming the appearance of an article in the *Science Citation Index* because it has been *cited* by another article rather than because it cites an earlier paper itself. In the latter role (citing paper rather than cited paper), it would appear much earlier.

TABLE 5

Ranked List of Sources Providing Information on Existence of a Research Project

Source of information on a research project	When project becomes accessible through this source	To whom accessibility is provided
1. The invisible college.	1. Conceivably before the research begins (i.e., at the proposal stage). In any event, no later than the commencement of the project.	1. First to the leaders in the field. Later to all others integrated into the invisible college.
2. The Smithsonian Science Information Exchange.	2. Shortly after the research grant is awarded.	2. To all individuals who make use of SSIE.
3. Technical reports.	3. Approximately 3 months after beginning of the project (assuming quarterly progress reports).	3. Members of the invisible college and others on distribution lists for these reports.
4. Indexes and abstracts of technical reports and other announcement devices from NTIS or other agencies responsible for the report literature.	4. Six months after the beginning of the project (assuming a quarterly progress report).	4. To all who make use of the report literature.
5. Professional conference.	5. Research methodology and, perhaps, preliminary results presented some 12 months after project begins.	5. To the invisible college. To all who attend the conference. To others who obtain preprints. To others who see the conference program and contact investigators.
6. Published listings of conference papers (e.g., *Current Programs*).	6. In an ideal situation, a conference program would be listed before the conference takes place. Frequently, however, the listing will occur concurrently with the meeting or possibly some months later.	6. To all who are aware of the existence of such listings, have access to them, and are willing to use them.

TABLE 5 (Continued)

Source of information on a research project	When project becomes accessible through this source	To whom accessibility is provided
7. Conference proceedings or conference preprints.	7. For some conferences, proceedings or preprints will be available at the time of the meeting or even before the meeting takes place. For others, however, the proceedings may not appear for many months or even years after the conference.	7. To all who attend the conference. To members of the invisible college. To others who learn of the existence of the paper and who contact the investigators.
8. Synopses of conferences.	8. Where such a synopsis is made (e.g., by an information analysis center), it should appear a few weeks after the conference itself.	8. To all who are aware of the existence of the synopsis.
9. The science journal.	9. A brief communication or letter may appear while the research project is still in progress, perhaps some 18 months after its initiation.	9. To those who scan the journal literature or who make use of *Current Cotents*.
10. Major indexing and abstracting services (covering journal literature) and machine-readable data bases derived from these services.	10. Some 6 months or more after the publication of the brief communication or letter. Under the best of conditions, it might be a little earlier. Under the worst of conditions, it might be much later. Some 2 years or more after the beginning of the project.	10. To all who make use of these secondary sources.
(11. The science journal.)	(11. Where no interim publication is made and the investigators wait for the conclu-	(11. To all who scan the journal literature or make use of *Current Contents*. To those

TABLE 5   (Continued)

Source of information on a research project	When project becomes accessible through this source	To whom accessibility is provided
	sion of the project before submitting a journal article, the current awareness mechanisms implied by 9 and 10 above will be delayed considerably. Perhaps the first full paper will appear 36 months after the project begins and it will become accessible through secondary sources some 6 months or more after that.)	who use appropriate secondary sources.)
12. Annual reviews.	12. Some 12 to 18 months after the appearance of the first journal article (perhaps 30 months after beginning of the research project). Earlier if the technical report literature is reviewed. Later if no interim publication appears in the journal literature.	12. To all who are aware of the existence of the annual review and who are willing to make use of it.
13. Citation of the research project, in the journal literature, by other writers.	13. Perhaps some 9 to 12 months after the original journal article is published. At best, perhaps some 27 months after inception of the project. At worst, very much later.	13. To those who read or scan the relevant journal literature.
14. Citation indexes.	14. Perhaps some 3 to 6 months after the appearance of the citation in the literature.	14. To all who use the *Science Citation Index*.

TABLE 5 (Continued)

Source of information on a research project	When project becomes accessible through this source	To whom accessibility is provided
15. Monographic literature.	15. Possibly 4 years or more after the beginning of the project and 2 years or more after its conclusion.	15. To those who receive announcements or advertising from publishers or who use various published bibliographies.

shows, in relation to the life history of the research project itself, at what point in time the source can provide access to the project and to whom access can be provided.

It is important to emphasize that the situation depicted in Figure 10, and summarized in Table 5, should be regarded as an optimum situation rather than a typical one. Throughout, the best circumstances have been assumed. The whole process of information dissemination through formal channels would be delayed if: The project is not reported to SSIE, there are no quarterly progress reports, there is no brief communication,

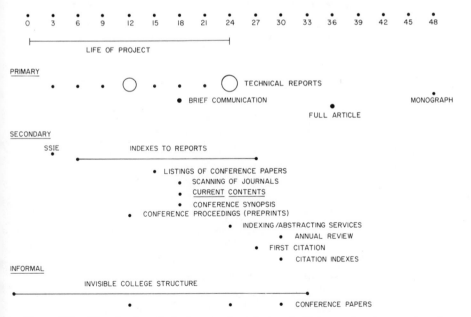

Figure 10. Life of a hypothetical research project and efficiency of various modes of transmitting information on the project. (The scale is in months.)

the report at a professional meeting is a complete report rather than an interim one, and so on. There is evidence to suggest that the typical situation is worse than the hypothetical one used as an example here. The subject has been discussed in detail by Garvey *et al.* (1970), Garvey and Griffith (1972), Lin *et al.* (1970), and Yokote and Utterback (1974).

The above discussion, of course, relates only to information from or about a formal research project. Not all publications result from formal research projects. In the case of an opinion paper or other "think" piece, as well as in the case of reports of practical experience (e.g., from industry, from health care), the journal may be the first practical means of dissemination to the scientific community. Even here, however, the informal channels of communication may have disseminated the substance of the paper to at least a chosen few.

In summary, we might say that an ideal scientific communication system would bring information on *ongoing research* to the attention of the science community at the earliest possible time. Mechanisms already exist to achieve this goal, at least for research in the United States. The mechanisms are the informal channels of communication, the Smithsonian Science Information Exchange, and the technical report literature. The science journal, however, is not an efficient current awareness mechanism, and secondary services based on the science journal are less current still. A scientist who relies solely on these mechanisms may keep "up to date" on scientific research of the immediate past but cannot be well informed on scientific research of the present.

There are, in fact, some very sound economic reasons for wanting to disseminate the results of science research, and information on the contents of ongoing or proposed research projects, at the earliest possible time. The more rapidly such information is disseminated, the greater the chance that undesirable duplication of research will be avoided and the greater the chance that current research will use the best available approaches, materials, and equipment. There is some evidence that the amount of undesirable duplication in science research is not inconsiderable. In a study of the value of two current awareness publications in the neurosciences, Lancaster (1974) found that 42.2% of the users of one publication (in a sample of 488 respondents) and 20.4% of the users of the second (sample of 509) claimed that the services had prevented duplication of research. Other savings in research time were reported by 34.2% and 40.5%, respectively, of the respondents to the two surveys. The evaluation of the Information Exchange Group experiments of the National Institutes of Health, as reported by Cooper (1968), revealed 346 cases in which the rapid dissemination mechanisms used in the experiments avoided duplication of research effort. In addition, there were 1111 cases in which the disseminated data changed the direction of a research project, 421 cases of savings in research time (with an estimate of 163 man-years saved), and 159 documented cases in which less expensive solutions to research problems were found (estimated saving of $523,000). The Information Exchange Group mechanism was reported to have disseminated research results, on the average, about 6 months earlier than the best of the other available mechanisms, and recipients of the service felt that this one source covered about 80% of the current research output relevant to their interests.

The best study of its kind, however, was that conducted by Martyn (1964) in England. In an investigation of 647 current research projects in government, industry, and academia, Martyn gathered documented evidence of 43 cases of unintentional duplication of research, and 106 cases in which information discovered from the literature, while research was underway, would, if found earlier, have saved time, money, or effort in the research project. Martyn found that in about 9% of all the projects studied, money could have been saved through an improved awareness of research reported in the literature. An extrapolation to the total expenditure for scientific research in the United Kingdom in 1962 (£640 million) led Martyn to conclude that at least £6 million a year could be saved in U.K. research through more effective use of the literature. This is likely to be a very low estimate, however, because it is based only on cases of duplication or suboptimum approaches to research discovered by the scientists through literature searches that were very probably quite incomplete. Martyn hypothesizes that this is only the tip of an iceberg and that much greater waste would be uncovered by more exhaustive searches of the literature. There is no real reason to suppose that the research situation in the United States is significantly better than that in the United Kingdom, in terms of effective exploitation of the results of earlier research. If Martyn's estimates of potential savings (about .9% of the total research budget) were anywhere close to being true of the U.S. situation at the present time, there could be economies of hundreds of millions of dollars a year through more effective and rapid dissemination of the results of scientific research.

The Problems of Libraries

Libraries have a very important role to play in the information transfer cycle depicted earlier in Figure 5 (p. 53). The great research libraries preserve the record of the achievements of science and technology as reflected in the published literature. These libraries assume the major responsibility for ensuring that research materials are available to scientists and other scholars when they are needed. Without the existence of such libraries, the progress of scientific investigation would be considerably impeded. The scientist would have no obvious source to go to for the record of scientific achievement of the past or for a wide selection of the scientific materials that are currently produced in published form. The existence in the United States, and in other developed countries, of many large and important research libraries tends to ensure that any science document of any value will be available, and will continue to be available from some source, and that serious gaps in coverage (and hence availability) are not allowed to occur.

It is obvious that the great research libraries (e.g., those in academic institutions) are posed great problems by the growth of the literature, by the increasing costs of publications, and by inexorably rising personnel costs. Table 6 presents some representative figures for the growth of 58 major research libraries in the United States. The figures are derived from Dunn *et al.* (1972). Table 6 indicates that, on the average, the libraries in this group grew approximately 37% in the 7-year period from 1965 to 1972, a mean annual growth of slightly over 5% a year. The rate of growth is rather erratic over the period, however, and in some years (e.g., 1969 and 1972) the rate of growth declined in relation to its rate in earlier years. The period 1965–1968 was one of general expansion. The years 1968–1972, however, show a much slower rate of growth. In the 7-year period, the mean operating expenditures increased by about 103% and the mean expenditures for materials and binding by 78%. It is important to note that the average cost of acquiring an item went up about 32% from 1965 to 1972. This figure, which includes various kinds of bibliographic materials, is simply derived by dividing the mean materials expenditures for this group of libraries by the mean number of volumes added each year.

Some comparison of these library figures, for growth and costs, with figures for publication growth and costs is of considerable interest. Some of these comparisons must, however, be made cautiously. We cannot, for example, directly compare the estimates for number of items published with estimates for growth of libraries, since the former figure represents number of *titles* and the latter number of *volumes*. There should, however, be a reasonable quantitative correlation between the two. That is, one might reasonably expect that the growth of the great research libraries, in number of volumes, should reasonably parallel the growth in the published literature measured in terms of new items.

One fact worth noting is that, at least in the period 1965–1972, the

TABLE 6

Selected Statistics from Fifty-Eight Major Research Libraries in the United States[a]

	1965	1966	1967	1968	1969	1970	1971	1972	Percentage of change 1965–1972
Mean holdings (number of volumes)	1,574,830	1,650,977	1,739,032	1,804,022	1,893,511	1,998,632	2,079,093	2,156,618	37
Mean number of volumes added	77,961	86,070	93,624	103,912	101,241	107,024	106,778	105,424	35
Mean total operating expenditures ($)	1,738,068	1,949,291	2,303,461	2,582,928	2,866,922	3,268,594	3,439,578	3,526,033	103
Mean expenditures for materials and bindings ($)	626,186	672,689	826,638	919,698	996,072	1,153,784	1,160,762	1,117,320	78
Average unit cost of acquisitions ($)[b]	8.03	7.82	8.83	8.85	9.84	10.78	10.87	10.60	32

[a] From Dunn, Tolliver, and Tolliver (1972) by permission of Purdue University Libraries.
[b] This figure is derived by dividing the mean materials expenditures for these libraries by the mean number of volumes added per year.

great research libraries seem to have grown at roughly the same rate as the published literature, despite individual aberrations from year to year. The number of new book titles and editions published in the United States has been increasing incrementally at an average annual rate of about 4.3%. In 1972 there was about 33% more new books published in the United States than in 1965. But, on the average, the academic libraries represented in Table 6 added 35% more volumes in 1972 than they did in 1965. These two figures are remarkably close and might suggest that, so far at least, the great academic libraries in the United States have been able to keep up reasonably well with the exponential growth of the published literature. It must be recognized, however, that the publication figure is based only on *book titles* but the library figure is based on *volumes* (including volumes of periodicals). The two figures are by no means comparable.

The figures of Table 6 have some very disquieting aspects. Most of the rate of growth reflected in Table 6 applies to an expansionary period from 1965 to 1968, coinciding with a period of general economic upswing in the country. The period 1968–1972, however, was a time in which the great libraries grew at a very much lower rate, falling far behind the rate of growth of the published literature. In 1972, for example, the 58 libraries were adding only 1.5% more items per year than they were in 1968. Yet, in the United States the production of new titles and new editions in science and technology was 20% greater in 1972 than it was in 1968. This seems to indicate that inflation in the publishing industry, as well as in library personnel costs, coupled with a period of economic stringency that has curtailed an adequate growth in library budgets, is now seriously threatening the ability of even the great research libraries to keep pace with the growth of the literature.

Table 6 indicates that, in the period 1965–1972, total expenditures of the great research libraries increased some 103% and materials and binding expenditures by some 78%. Yet the collections grew in size by only 37% in this period. Unfortunately, this is indicative of the fact that library service tends to be a very labor-intensive activity, and that the publishing industry, on which library services depend, is also extremely labor-intensive. Neither of these industries has as yet benefited appreciably from automation activities. Library budgets, although they are growing steadily, are not increasing at a rate adequate to compensate for increases in certain publication costs. The average price of a hardcover book published in the United States increased some 59% from 1965 to 1973, but the average cost of a periodical subscription went up some 133% in this same period and the average cost of a periodical subscription in science increased over 150%. Moreover, in certain fields of science the rate of increase has been well above this average—over 200% in 8 years in chemistry, physics, and engineering. But, as Table 6 indicates, library budgets have grown only 103% in the period 1965–1972, and materials budgets even less than this. It is clear that this rate of growth, although impressive, is not adequate to compensate for both the growth of the literature and increasing costs of the literature, especially for purchases in science and technology, and that the great academic and research libraries, as suggested by Baumol and Marcus (1973), Leimkuhler and Neville (1967), and Salton (1975), among others, may indeed be reaching a crisis. The crisis is one caused by lack of continued financial support adequate to sustain the growth of collections at a rate comparable to the growth of the published literature and, at the same time, to compensate for the continual spiral of publication costs. Because of the labor-intensive nature of library activities, a large part of the growth in library budgets has to be absorbed by increased personnel and other administrative costs, and less and less money is available for materials. This is reflected in the figures mentioned earlier: Academic library budgets increased 103% in 7 years, while materials and binding budgets increased only 78% in the same period, and the rate at which materials were added grew a mere 37%. The increase in personnel budgets, moreover, seems to be going mainly into salary increases to present staff rather than to an expansion of existing staffs and thus to the provision of additional capabilities or services.

A valuable analysis of the economics of academic libraries in the United States has been published by Baumol and Marcus (1973). Their data are derived from the Purdue University collection of data for 58 research libraries, from which the data of Table 6 are taken, covering the period of 1950–1951 to 1968–1969. Baumol and Marcus point out that the larger, more well established libraries are growing more slowly than the relatively smaller libraries (3.5% per annum growth as compared with a 5.4% per annum growth), and that all libraries in the group will tend to equalize the size of their collections in time. The difference in size between the largest libraries and the smallest libraries is now being reduced at a rate of about 2% per annum. Over the entire period covered in the Baumol and Marcus study, the number of volumes added annually has been growing at a rate of about 7% a year. By 1990, they project, the rate of growth will have quadrupled (i.e., four times as many volumes will be added in 1990 as were added in 1950).

An approximate measure of the effect of inflation on acquisitions costs is reflected in the difference between rate of increase in materials expenditures and rate of increase in volumes added. For example, the 58 libraries added only 35% more volumes in 1972 than they did in 1965, although their materials budgets were 78% greater. Baumol and Marcus show that, from 1950–1951 to 1968–1969, average library expenditures increased by more than 10% per annum but inputs to the library (of materials and staff) increased only 5 to 7%, the difference being absorbed by rising personnel and materials costs. The library cost per student, however, has been growing at about the same rate as the total educational cost per student. The size of the professional staff of academic libraries grew in the period covered by the Baumol and Marcus study but it has actually declined in relation to (a) the number of students served, (b) the number of volumes held, (c) the number of volumes added, and (d) the size of the nonprofessional staff, smaller libraries showing a more rapid rate of relative decline.

Per unit library costs have been growing much faster than general price levels as exemplified by the Wholesale Price Index (see Figure 11). From 1951 to 1969 the cost per student for the operations of a university library went up at an annual rate of slightly over 6%, while the Wholesale Price Index increased at an annual rate of less than 1% in the same period. The fact that the library cost per student has been growing at over 6% per annum while costs associated with computer processing have been steadily declining (see Figure 12), leads Baumol and Marcus

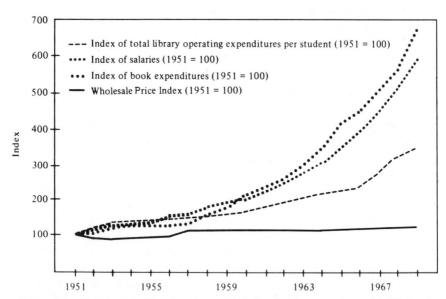

Figure 11. Unit costs in 58 university research libraries in comparison with Wholesale Price Index, 1951–1969. (From Baumol and Marcus, 1973 by permission of the American Council on Education.)

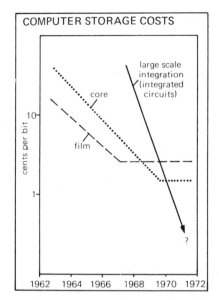
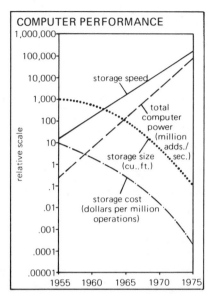

Figure 12. Indices of costs and performance in computer processing. (From McHale, 1972 by permission of the Conference Board.)

to the conclusion that increased automation is inevitable in academic libraries if they are to survive. Baumol and Marcus also highlight the labor-intensive nature of library activities. The cost of labor is rising at comparable rates in the manufacturing industries and in the service industries. But labor requirements fall cumulatively and steadily in one sector and remain fairly constant in the other, leading to an inevitable differential in cost behavior. The costs of the service sector, including libraries, must rise steadily and cumulatively relative to those elsewhere in the economy at a percentage rate directly related to the differential in their productivity. If total wages increase at 5% a year, productivity in manufacturing increases by 4% a year, but productivity in the service sector remains relatively constant, the cost of manufactured goods will go up at an annual rate of 1% but those of services will rise at 5%. Since libraries are labor-intensive, and productivity has tended to remain relatively constant, the economic situation in libraries is not likely to improve unless a much wider use of automation, preferably through cooperative projects among libraries, is adopted in order to raise substantially present levels of productivity and lower unit costs of operation.

The phenomenon of increasing library budgets with relatively declining power for the purchase of materials, highlighted by Baumol and Marcus

(1973), is further substantiated by later data from the Fry and White (1975) study. Fry and White investigated the interaction between economic factors affecting publishing and economic factors affecting the provision of library service. They concluded that the economic system, in which publishers of scholarly journals are becoming more and more dependent on institutional subscriptions, is becoming increasingly a closed and unstable one: "The need which publishers have to secure revenues from libraries is simply not matched by the ability of libraries to supply those revenues from their own budgets. Left to its own devices, this unstable economic system could lead to a disastrous downward spiral of lowered subscriptions leading to higher prices leading in turn to lowered subscriptions, ad infinitum |p. 6|."

Some Achievements of the Last Decade

Since this chapter has given considerable attention to the major problems of scientific and technical communication, it seems appropriate to summarize as well some of the achievements of the last decade.

As mentioned in Chapter 2, the most significant events in information processing since 1960 have been the development of machine-readable data bases and the use of on-line access to exploit these files most effectively. The application of computers to the publication of secondary services has had a number of important benefits. First, there is little doubt that printed indexes and abstracts journals would now cost even more if they were not produced with the benefit of machine aid. One of the great advantages of producing a data base in machine-readable form is that, from a single indexing and input operation, it is possible to generate a number of products and services, including published indexes, SDI, and retrospective search services. The National Library of Medicine (NLM), for example, generates a data base from which *Index Medicus* is printed; many specialized bibliographies in various branches of medicine are automatically generated at regular intervals, SDI services are provided, and retrospective searches are undertaken. The production by NLM of its "recurring bibliography" series is one example of an innovative application of computers to the publication of printed indexes. These specialized bibliographies are created through the use of stored search strategies (rather like SDI profiles) which retrieve the citations of potential interest to various segments of the medical community. These citations are then spun off onto tapes from which special bibliographies of relevance to dentistry, nursing, rheumatology, toxicology, endocrinology, and other special fields, are published at regular intervals.

As reported in Chapter 2, the growth of machine-readable data bases has been quite phenomenal. From 1965 to 1978 the number of digital files from which various information services could be provided increased from one to something in excess of 500. The growth of machine-readable data bases, coupled with networking arrangements for making these accessible, has greatly increased the availability of information services. This can be demonstrated by using the National Library of Medicine example once more. In 1965, when the MEDLARS retrospective search service was just beginning, virtually all of the expertise in searching this data base was concentrated in a handful of search analysts on the staff of NLM itself, and the volume of searches that could be conducted in the United States was severely limited, perhaps to something on the order of 3000 a year. When the MEDLARS off-line network was fully developed, at the end of the decade, the situation had considerably improved. Through the establishment of a network of regional MEDLARS centers, and through the training of information specialists on the staff of these centers, the number of qualified MEDLARS analysts increased considerably, to perhaps 50 active searchers, and the number of searches handled in the United States rose to about 20,000 a year. The move to on-line processing, in the 1970s, further improved the situation by an order of magnitude. In 1975 there were about 300 MEDLINE centers operating in the United States, the number of trained searchers had increased to perhaps 500, and the number of searches conducted had grown to about 20,000 each month in the United States alone, with many additional searches occurring elsewhere in the world.

The increasing accessibility of information services, as demonstrated in the MEDLARS example, has a very favorable effect on their economics since the economics of information services is very volume-dependent. In 1967 a realistic estimate of the cost of one MEDLARS search was $150 when personnel costs, machine costs, and a portion of the costs of creating the data base (the remainder being allocated to the published indexes) were allocated to the retrospective search function (Cummings, 1967). In 1977, 10 years later, the average cost of a MEDLINE search in the United States was down to perhaps one-tenth of this. Thus, in the case of this data base at least, the cost per machine search has declined dramatically within a decade.

Some idea of the growth of machine literature searching in the United States can be obtained from Figure 13. The diagram, which relates only to on-line, interactive searches, shows an increase from a handful of searches before 1966 to 700,000 a year by 1974 and a projection to over a million by 1975. In actual fact it is estimated that some 2 million on-line searches were conducted in 1977. The exploitation of machine-

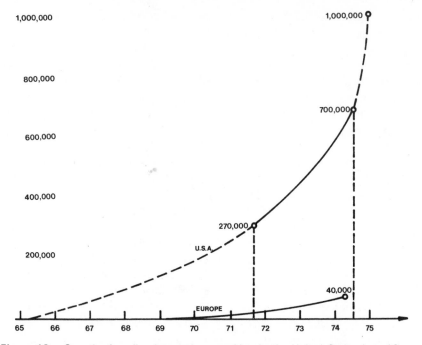

Figure 13. Growth of on-line interactive searching in the United States in a 10-year period. (Figures prepared by Martha Williams, University of Illinois, and reproduced with her permission. This diagram first appeared in NEWSIDIC, the information bulletin of the European Association of Scientific Information Dissemination Centers, October, 1974.)

readable files interactively in Europe began later but had picked up considerable momentum by 1976. Pratt (1975) identified over 300 different data bases and data banks, many of U.S. origin, now being used in the provision of information services in Europe. Williams and Brandhorst (1976) were able to identify 277 data bases which collectively provided access to over 52 million records, of which about 33 million were estimated to be accessible on-line. In addition, they mention the existence of another 200 data bases for which no data on file sizes were available. Figure 14 is a projection of the growth, in number of uses and number of users, of on-line information services in Europe in the period 1976 to 1983. Accessibility of data bases in Europe will be greatly improved in the near future by EURONET, SCANNET, and other networking arrangements.

King et al. (1976) estimated that the average cost of an on-line search in the United States declined from about $1000 in 1968 to about $70 in 1975. Although these estimates seem rather high, they nevertheless give a reasonable indication of the magnitude of the reductions in machine searching costs during this period, due to reduced costs of machine processing, more efficient and less costly telecommunications, and spreading of data base investment over a greater volume of uses. In 1977 Bibliographic Retrieval Services was quoting on-line connect costs as low as $10 per hour for high volume users (about 80 hours per month). For use of data bases for which no royalties are charged, these rates bring the cost of an average on-line search down to something in the neighborhood of $2.50 to $3.50, exclusive of terminal rental or purchase costs (minimal when amortized over many searches), the time of the searcher, and cost of printing citations off-line. Even with a royalty charge of $15 per connect hour, the total on-line costs for a search could be as low as $5.75 to $8.50.

Another aspect of the economics of information services is worth mentioning. On-line processing makes large data bases available to

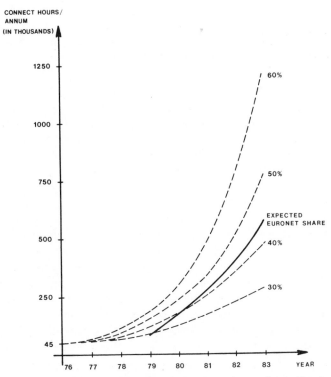

Figure 14. On-line searching in Europe based on assumed annual growth rates of 30%, 40%, 50%, 60%. (Prepared by H. Ungerer, Commission of the European Communities, and reproduced with his permission.)

many organizations and individuals who could not otherwise afford convenient access. Consider the case of a small industrial library for which chemistry is a subject of peripheral rather than central interest. It would probably be uneconomical for this library to subscribe to the printed *Chemical Abstracts* at $3,500 a year. At a level of demand of, say, three searches each month, the "access cost" for the printed data base would work out to be approximately $100 a search. It is considerably cheaper to buy on-line access when the need for a search in the data base arises. It is only when the volume of searches in *Chemical Abstracts* approaches 150 a year that the data base investment costs for the printed version begin to approach the costs of purchasing on-line access when the need for service arises. Moreover, the on-line search will be more efficient, rapid, and thorough than a comparable search in the printed index. Some types of searches will only be practical in the machine data base because they are too complex to handle manually (too many terms in too many combinations) or involve the use of access points that exist in the digital files but not in the printed indexes.

Machine-readable data bases and on-line processing have *greatly* improved the accessibility of information resources and have practically eliminated geographic distance as a barrier to information flow. In the world of electronic communications, the small library can have access to the same range of machine-readable files as the largest information centers. A one-man hospital library in a small town can use a terminal to exploit the MEDLINE data base as well as a number of more specialized files in medicine, thus giving the doctor associated with this hospital literature searching capabilities more sophisticated and more comprehensive than he has ever had before. It would be true to say, in fact, that the accessibility of information resources in on-line, machine-readable form is increasing at least as rapidly as the accessibility of these resources in their printed form is declining.

Machine-readable data bases also have some impact on the timeliness of secondary services since the machine-readable version of an index is likely to be available some weeks before the printed version to which it relates. This is particularly valuable in the dissemination of information internationally. The monthly update of a machine-readable file may be flown from the United States to, say, Australia to arrive days or even hours after it is available for use in the United States and some months before the printed analog reaches Australia. International on-line connections can speed up this process even more.

In comparison with its impact on secondary publications, the computer has had comparatively little influence as yet on the publishing of primary journals in science. True, some science journals are photocomposed and thus exist in machine-readable form at some point. But a very small proportion of the world's science journals is produced in this way, and little attempt has been made to use the digital journal text for other products or services. As far as is known, there are no journals issued solely in digital form, although a small number are issued as microfiche only. Kuney (1973) indicated that by the end of 1970 there were well over 1200 computer typesetting installations in the United States, but only a very small number of these are used to produce primary journals. The majority are used in newspaper production. One of the problems, of course, is that the small organizations typical of much scientific publishing are unable to afford the capital investment needed to implement computerized operations. Moreover, their scale of operation is likely to be too small for efficient mechanization. A possible solution to these problems, as described by Bamford (1973), is the Editorial Processing Center, a mechanism for combining small publishing operations (without loss of individual editorial control) in order to achieve the scale of operation needed to apply computerization efficiently and economically.

Referring once more to Figure 5 (p. 53), we can say that considerable progress has been made in the application of computers to steps 7 and 9 of the communication cycle, and some progress has been applied in the mechanization of the library activities of steps 5 and 6. It is likely that substantial future progress can only come from automation applied to the remaining steps in the cycle. This implies the distribution of secondary publications electronically and, later, the production and distribution of primary publications in electronic form.

In the remainder of the book we will consider a possible configuration for a completely electronic system in science that would be comparable to the intelligence system described earlier. In such a system, all aspects of formal communication, including primary publishing, would be conducted in a paperless mode.

6

Scenario for an Electronic
Information System for
the Year 2000

So far in this book we have examined some major improvements in the dissemination and retrieval of information realized since 1963, have discussed the problems existing in the present communication cycle, and have described progress toward completely paperless systems in the intelligence community. The remaining chapters, which are intended to be read as a unit, deal with a possible future for information transfer in science and technology. This chapter presents a scenario for a future system, largely from the viewpoint of the scientist user. Economic feasibility and cost-benefit considerations are addressed in Chapter 7, problems of implementation in Chapter 8, and the role of the library in a paperless environment is discussed in Chapter 9.

It seems appropriate to illustrate the possible characteristics of a paperless system for scientific communication by presenting a scenario for a system as it might exist at some time in the future. I have chosen the year 2000 as the date of the scenario, but a system along the lines described might in fact be implemented much earlier.

In the electronic communication system envisaged, every scientist will have an on-line terminal in his office. Perhaps he will also have one in his home. The terminal will be likely to have some form of video display to receive information, and some form of keyboard to transmit information. The video display might consist of a CRT device, a plasma panel, or some other display mechanism yet to be invented. The keyboard may be only one of several communication devices available with the terminal. Some forms of communication may be achieved by light pen, by finger touch, or other mechanisms. These are technological considerations that must eventually be addressed but which are unimportant in the present scenario.

The scientist will use his terminal, routinely on a daily basis, for three major functions:

1. To create information
2. To transmit information
3. To receive information

The word *information* is used loosely and implies here a wide range of communication media, including numerical data, text in paragraph form, diagrams, and so on. The terminal is the scientist's entry to a vast communication network without geographic bounds. It can connect him with other individuals to permit conversational interaction, or it can connect him with an almost infinite variety of data bases and data banks.

More specifically, the scientist of the future will use his terminal to receive text, to compose text, to search for text, to seek the answers to factual questions, to build information files, and to converse with colleagues. The terminal will provide a single point of entry to a wide range of capabilities that will substitute, wholly or in part, for many activities that are now handled in different ways: the writing of letters, the receipt of mail, the composition and distribution of research reports, the receipt of science journals, the collection of documents in personal files, the searching of library catalogs and printed indexes, the searching of handbooks of scientific data, visits to libraries and other information centers, and even certain types of professional "conversations" now conducted through the telephone or face-to-face encounter.

We can reasonably assume that the scientist will use his terminal as a type of electronic notebook in which he records details and observations on his ongoing research. These informal notes, giving background to the study, equipment, and methodology used, results achieved, and interpretation of these results, can be entered at any time into a designated "ongoing project file." It is from these informal notes that the scientist will construct his research reports. The reports themselves, both the reports he may be required to submit regularly to a sponsoring agency and those he wishes to make more widely known through some formal publication process, will be written at the terminal. In the process of composition, the author will of course draw from the notes he has been compiling in his electronic notebook. He will also have available some rather sophisticated text editing programs, which will make it very simple to make alterations in his text—transposition of sentences or paragraphs, deletions and corrections, and even the wholesale substitution of one word for another throughout the report (needed, for example, if he discovers that he has consistently misspelled a particular word). In addition, he can expect to have available various on-line reference tools, including dictionaries and data banks of various kinds, which will make the task of accurate reporting so much easier. Presumably too, he will have the capability of electronically copying into his own report any quotations, tables, or bibliographic references that he wishes to take from reports already accessible in machine-readable files. In an electronic environment, the problems of checking bibliographic references will be an order of magnitude more simple than is true at present.

When the scientist is reasonably satisfied with what he has written, he may decide that he would like to have his report reviewed, in an informal way, by some of his professional colleagues. He will submit the draft of his text to these colleagues, within his own institution or far beyond it, electronically. This may mean that the text is copied from his personal files (which no one else may access) into some controlled access file. A message, addressed to those colleagues who are to review the report, is put into the communication system. The message asks these individuals if they would examine the draft and gives them the information (including a password) that will allow them to access the text. When one of these scientists next goes into a "mail scan" mode at his terminal (which could conceivably be seconds after the message is entered) he will see the message and, when ready to do so, call up the text for examination. The comments of the reviewers are transmitted to the author in the same way.

The author, of course, may choose to modify his report (I hesitate to use the word *paper* in this context!) on the basis of the comments received. When it reaches its final form, the report may be transmitted electronically to its final destination. This may be the files of a sponsoring agency or it may be the publisher of some electronic journal.

The publication of primary literature in the year 2000 may in fact be a more or less direct electronic analog of the present system. Descriptions of ongoing research projects will get into on-line files similar to those now maintained by the Smithsonian Science Information Exchange. Patents will be stored in machine-readable patent files, dissertations in dissertation files, standards in standards files, and so on. Unreferred technical reports would be accessible through data bases maintained by government agencies and other sponsors of research. Science "journals" would continue to be published by professional societies and commercial enterprises. By this I mean that these organizations would build machine-readable data bases, in special subject areas, that would be roughly comparable to the present packaging of articles into printed journals. Thus, one can visualize the existence of an applied physics file maintained by the American Institute of Physics, a heat transfer file maintained by the American Society of Mechanical Engineers, and so on. It is entirely conceivable that an author may match certain characteristics of his paper (e.g., keywords in title and/or abstract) against a machine-stored index to primary data bases in order to decide which publisher is most likely to be interested. The paper is submitted to the publisher along with an "electronic" letter of submission. Refereeing would continue, but all communication among referees, authors, and editors would take place electronically. The allocation of reports to referees could be handled more efficiently through on-line directories of referees, through automatic scheduling and follow-up procedures, and perhaps through some profile matching algorithm which allocates each report to those available referees whose interests and experience coincide most closely with the scope of a particular article.

Acceptance of an article into a public data base implies that the article has satisfied the scientific review process and received the "endorsement" of the publisher. In the electronic world, however, space considerations are less likely to be a major constraint on how much is accepted for publication. This may mean that more articles can be accepted by the first source to which they are submitted by authors, resulting in greatly reduced delays in making research results widely accessible. It may also mean that acceptance for publication need no longer involve a binary decision. Instead, as Roistacher (1978) suggests, the refereeing process may lead to the allocation of some type of numerical score to a paper, the score reflecting the judgment of the referees on the value of the contribution. Every article having a score above some pre-set value would be accepted into the data base, the score being carried along with the article. Even the articles falling below the required value might, with the permission of the authors, be accepted into a second-level data base. Once the articles become accessible to the scientific community at large, a form of "public refereeing" becomes possible. The system itself can record the degree of use that a particular item receives, readers can assign their own weights to an article, using some standard scale, and they can place their comments (anonymous or signed) into a public comment file, with comments linked to the identifying numbers of articles. The electronic system, then, may allow an author whose contribution received a low initial rating from his referees to be "vindicated" by the reaction of the wider community of scientists. If the composition is accepted for publication, it will be added to the data base of this particular publisher. It will not need to be keyboarded again, although the publisher may want to make further editorial corrections or other alterations before he adds it to his file. "Publication" implies releasing it to the public. This may mean that the publisher designates the publication as belonging to a particular segment of the file roughly corresponding to the characteristics of a conventional journal. For example, if the publisher is the American Psychological Association, certain compositions might go into a "child psychology" file, others into a "psychoanalysis" file, and so on. A multifaceted paper may go into more than one of these files, which would be roughly equivalent to putting it into several conventional journals, because it will not cost significantly more to duplicate papers among data bases. The files thus created could obviously be used to print issues of conventional journals if printed journals still have a role to play in such a communication system (e.g., for archival purposes). It is more likely, however, that print on paper will disappear completely in this application and that the journals will exist only in digital form.[1]

As suggested in the preceding discussion, the processes by which an article is submitted, reviewed, and accepted for publication may not be radically different in the year 2000 than they are in 1978. It seems more likely, however, that a paperless system may force rather sweeping changes in the way that the science literature is distributed and paid for. It would certainly seem undesirable if the distribution procedures of the electronic system are more or less direct equivalents of the present situation. If a scientist is expected to subscribe for the privilege of accessing one or two data bases, a major defect of the present system—the rather inefficient way in which reports of science research are packaged—would simply be perpetuated. Obviously preferable would be some immense SDI service through which a scientist is automatically notified of any new report, added to any accessible data base, that

---

[1] It is not quite clear who it was that first discussed the possibility of a paperless journal. Sondak and Schwarz (1973) mentioned the possibility and visualized journals receiving machine-readable input from authors and using on-line displays for all reviewing and editorial processes. Libraries would receive an "archival file" in machine-readable form but individual subscribers would receive the journal on microfiche, this form being produced by COM (Computer Output Micro-film) procedures. Clearly, this proposal could only be regarded as an interim measure, dictated solely by the fact that not all potential users now have on-line display devices readily accessible to them. It is interesting to note that Sondak and Schwarz, writing in 1973, predicted that paperless journals would be commonplace within a decade.

matches a stored profile of his interests. He may go into an "SDI mode" at any time of any day to discover items disseminated to him within a specified time period (e.g., the past week) from any source. It is likely that this dissemination will be handled in a number of stages. Probably the scientist will view citations first or, possibly, citations plus abstracts. If he sees items of interest, he may then access the full text of the papers.

The implementation of a global SDI service of this kind is technologically feasible right now, but it raises major questions relating to organization, administration, and division of responsibility. How many SDI services should exist in the electronic environment and who should manage and maintain them? It would certainly seem inefficient if each publisher of primary data bases must maintain his own SDI program. Perhaps this function would become a prime responsibility of the present publishers of secondary services. Thus we might expect to see the emergence of national and international on-line SDI services based upon discipline-oriented and mission-oriented secondary data bases.

The individual user would be billed for the amount of SDI service he receives, the great size of the population served bringing the cost per individual down to a figure that could become rather insignificant. The SDI services used would bring the scientist citations, and perhaps abstracts, of new literature (from all types of sources) matching his interest profile. For each item brought to his attention in this way, the system will be able to provide, on request, an indication of how he can access the full text and how much it will cost to access it. If the scientist chooses to access the complete text of any item, which would be maintained in the files of a primary publisher, he must presumably pay for the privilege of doing so. The paperless communication system is likely to be a much more "pay as you go" one, with an individual paying for just as much as he chooses to use rather than subscribing to conventional journal packages, a large part of the contents of which may not be directly relevant to his interests.

The secondary publisher would presumably continue to be involved in the indexing and abstracting of the primary literature, although most of the abstracts would simply be those provided by authors and primary publishers. All indexing, of course, will be carried out on-line (which implies the need for dual-screen terminals). The "scope" of a secondary data base, however, would no longer be defined in terms of a list of journals (or other sources) covered. Instead, one foresees the need for various levels of SDI within the communication system. The interest profiles (gigantic ones) of the secondary publishers would be matched against updates of primary data bases so that items of potential interest would be disseminated to these secondary services rapidly and auto-matically. Perhaps science libraries, and other types of information centers, will acquire their document collections in much the same way. The customers of the secondary publishers, and/or of libraries and other information centers, would in turn have their interest profiles matched regularly against the data bases of these institutions. There might also be cooperation among the secondary services so that the "first one in " is responsible for preparing abstract and citation in a standard format, although some form of automatic descriptive cataloging is also possible. This, of course, is just one possible "model" for a dissemination system of the future. The model may seem a rather radical departure from the ways in which primary publishers, secondary publishers and libraries now operate. But, if we are indeed moving into an electronic age, such radical departures from tradition are almost inevitable.

The individual scientist, then, can have his interest profile matched regularly against one or more SDI services operated by secondary publishers or by some form of information center. These services, to which he or his institution subscribes, will draw his attention continuously to new literature of all types—research reports, journal arti-cles, dissertations, patents, standards, regulations—corresponding to his current professional interests. The word *continuously* is used deliberately because this is viewed as an operation in which the scientist can reasonably expect to get a few things each day in his mail, rather than receiving a much larger output at weekly or monthly intervals.

Any item for which the scientist has no use can be disposed of immediately simply by depressing an appropriate key. Items that appear to be of some interest can be pursued at once. Alternatively, the scientist may choose to read off the bibliographic data into his own private electronic files for later action. An item viewed in its entirety can also be placed into private files in much the same way that an article may be photocopied and placed in the paper files of an individual. In the electronic world, the machine-readable file of resources replaces the paper file. But in the private electronic file, an item can be indexed in any way desired, and with as many access points as the user wishes. The paperless personal file will have infinitely greater search capabilities than the paper files it replaces, and it will occupy virtually no space (since, conceptually at least, a report need exist physically in only one file, its "existence" in other files being achieved through the use of pointers to master files of primary text). The scientist may also evaluate any report that he examines. Personal notes or comments will go into his own electronic files. If he wishes to make "public" comments, these will go into some form of publicly accessible comments file. Thus a user who calls up a particular paper may ask to see any public comments associated with this paper.

The scientist will use his terminal for current awareness purposes. At the terminal he will view items of all kinds disseminated to him from all kinds of sources—from primary publishers, from secondary publishers, from work associates, and from professional colleagues located at other institutions. Professional correspondence will be handled through this network and conversational interaction will also take place on-line. Among the materials thus disseminated to the scientist will be research proposals, abstracts of ongoing research, "journal articles," research reports, conference papers, information on forthcoming conferences, patents, standards, and specifications. He or his institution will pay for the amount of service requested and received from the system. In contrast to the current journal situation, the scientist will be likely to pay only for the materials relevant to his interests.

So far we have mostly considered input to an electronic communication system, dissemination of items within this system, and the building of files of these items. The scientist will also need to search for information—both factual data and text describing particular phenomena of interest. At present, the scientist will seek information of this kind through his own personal files or through conversations with colleagues or consultants. Sometimes (but frequently as a last resort) he will visit a library or other formal information center. In the electronic system, all of these approaches to information seeking may be conducted through the same terminal. The terminal, of course, gives him access to his own information files (and possibly, the information files maintained by some of his colleagues or by his department). If these files fail him, his terminal will provide an entry point to a vast array of outside sources. Accessible to him on-line will be machine-readable files that are the electronic equivalents of printed handbooks, directories, dictionaries, encyclopedias, almanacs, and other reference tools. He will also have access to on-line indexes to primary text, presumably built and maintained by those same organizations that provide his SDI service. The scientist will be able to use a "widening horizons" approach to his information seeking in this environment, going from personal files to institutional files to national and international resources. And any useful item of data, or piece of text, that he uncovers during his search can, of course, be added rather easily to his personal information files.

Files of numerical and statistical data (i.e., data banks), as well as text, will be available. When the need for information arises, then, the scientist can go to his terminal and put in his request in natural language form. This is then matched against an on-line referral center which tells him which data bases are most likely to satisfy his inquiry, and how much it will cost to interrogate these services. When he has selected a particular file he calls this up and interrogates it. Preferably he should be able to do this in English sentence form. At the very least, the system should be capable of leading him tutorially into the construction of a correct search strategy. Communication of this type, to satisfy a particular information need, may involve on-line conversation with another individual (e.g., a specialist at an information analysis center) rather than communication with a data base. Geographic distance will be no obstacle to communication in such a system since a data base 5000 miles away can be queried as easily as one 10 miles away, and perhaps at no more cost. The electronic information system of the year 2000 will have a built-in document delivery capability. The full digital text of any item will be stored in designated centers from which the individual user can request that it be transferred for viewing at his own station. For high-quality graphic material, however, it may be necessary to use microform stores that can be interfaced with the digital storage system.

Finally, the on-line communications network will greatly improve the possibilities for informal communication since scientists will be able to exchange materials freely within the system and will be able to conduct conversations, by terminal, with other scientists, even those in remote locations. On-line directories will provide names and address codes for scientists and these will be indexed by personal and institutional names, geographic location, subject interests and expertise, and other characteristics. It is possible that the need for professional conferences, in their present form, may be greatly reduced in such a system because small groups of scientists will be able to arrange their own specialized "teleconferences" using the facilities provided by the on-line communications networks.

Symbiosis between Formal and Informal Channels

It seems very likely that the distinction between formal and informal communication will be much less clear in an all-electronic environment. The user terminal will provide access to informal as well as formal channels. Ideally, a modern information service in a scientific field should:

1. Facilitate rapid and effective person-to-person and group-to-group communications
2. Maintain indexes to ongoing research and make these highly accessible

3. Make the "archival" literature of science as accessible as possible
4. Provide facilities to aid the scientist in building and exploiting his own information files
5. Provide rapid and convenient access to the facilities of one or more information analysis centers

In the past, it has never been possible to meld these various characteristics and components into a single, cohesive structure. They have tended to exist as separate, although related and overlapping, activities. In the last quarter of the twentieth century, however, it should be entirely possible to integrate these activities within a single, cohesive system.

The value of the invisible colleges, and the desirability of extending these social structures to embrace a larger number of participants, has been recognized for some time. The most important work in this area, the Information Exchange Group (IEG) experiment of the National Institutes of Health, (see, for example, Heenan and Weeks, 1971), had as its objective the expansion of existing invisible college structures in biomedicine. Each chairman of an IEG deliberately sought to bring into the group all scientists active in the research area, and NIH itself provided the duplication and mailing support to allow any communication, generated by any group member, to go rapidly and simultaneously to every other member of the group. But the IEG experiment was conducted at a time when the only feasible means of duplication and dissemination was print-on-paper and the mails. Now we need no longer be bound by these mechanisms. On-line computer technology, and in particular the use of on-line systems for computer conferencing (see Price, 1975), opens up completely new dimensions in interpersonal and intergroup communications. An IEG experiment conducted now could be very much different from one conducted in the 1960s.

In a largely electronic world, how might the informal channels of communication interact profitably and efficiently with the more formal channels, as exemplified, let us say, by the information analysis centers (IACs)? Let us first make the assumption that some IAC exists in a particular subject field and that some type of invisible college structure can be identified in the same field. It would be the task of the IAC to identify, as completely as possible, all the scientists working in this area of research. It would be its second task, using techniques similar to those of Crawford (1971), to identify the existing patterns of communications within this research community and, in particular, to identify the sociometric stars or "central scientists." Once this is done, the objectives of the IAC should be to "capture" the communications of the invisible college, to make these more widely available, to enlarge the communication network by bringing in further scientists, and to provide the telecom-munications–computer support structure to allow the more effective dissemination and exploitation of information resources within the com-munity as a whole.

What can be visualized is a computer conferencing network established in a research area with the appropriate IAC as the hub of the network. The network might be quite small at first, embracing a few key centers in the United States, but would grow quite rapidly and eventually become completely international. The IAC must, of course, provide the facilities needed to enlarge the network and to make communication among the members more rapid and convenient. It must also provide facilities to assist the work of the scientist members and be able to demonstrate the value of these facilities, so that the benefits of membership in the communication network are shown to clearly out-weigh any "costs" to the individual members. Facilities provided by the IAC will include computer storage, network access, and message routing, indexing of communications, support of the building and exploitation of personal files on-line, and access to relevant machine-readable files built by the IAC and other organizations. The IAC must have the necessary computer resources to support an on-line network of the type proposed. Conceivably, however, a single computer facility could support a whole group of IACs, and their associated communications networks (e.g., a group of such networks in the energy field).

It is assumed that every participating scientist, or research group, has an on-line terminal as point of access to the network. It is also assumed that this terminal can be used to communicate directly with other scientists or groups, to put messages into the system (a kind of electronic "memorandum to file") although not directed to anyone in particular, to receive messages, to build and exploit personal files, and to access machine-readable data bases or data banks made available by the IAC. For many purposes, of course, use of the network facilities must be considered "public" and any item put into the network should be considered generally accessible to the IAC and to the other network par-ticipants. Certain activities, however, while supported by the network facilities, may be kept confidential. It must, for example, be possible to maintain the confidentiality of the information files built by individual scientists for their own use.

Scientists will be expected to "compose" their research reports and memoranda (including drafts of papers to be presented at conferences or to be submitted to science journals) at their on-line terminals. The net-work will provide text editing and other facilities to aid in this task. At the composition stage, the work of a scientist is completely confidential.

The network merely gives him the necessary storage and machine support facilities to aid in the composition. Once the composition phase is over, however, and the scientist is ready to "transmit" (i.e., he is willing to have others see his work), the communication becomes a "network communication" and is stored by the network in an accessible form. The network communication file, which will reflect truly current research in the field, will grow rapidly. It will include informal memoranda directed to the network in general, memoranda directed to particular members, and drafts of more formal communications (conference papers, journal articles, research reports). The IAC will maintain on-line directories of network members, with communication codes, to facilitate the transmission of communications among members.

The network communications will be stored in the IAC computer facilities. The IAC staff may catalog and index the communications to facilitate future retrieval. The communications themselves will be presented in a standard format. When a scientist wishes to enter a communication into the network, he calls up a communications "format" at his on-line terminal. This format will include fields for identification of author, of destination (if sent to a particular individual), of title, of date, and of free keywords. These data form a basic cataloging record which can be added to or modified by the IAC staff at a later time. For identification purposes a unique control number will be assigned to each communication.

For current awareness purposes, a scientist can make use of the network in a number of different ways:

1. He uses his terminal to receive all communications directed specifically to him by other network members. Such communications are likely to come with an "attached" message.
2. He can "browse" among the "catalog records" for all communications added to the network within a specified period of time (i.e., those added since he was last in a browse mode).
3. He can construct a search strategy (which he can store as an SDI user interest profile) in order to find all recent communications that match his special interests. An important element in such a profile will be the serial numbers of communications in which he is specially interested. These numbers will lead him directly to all later communications that refer to those known to represent his interests.

Searching the files of research communications can be achieved on the basis of keywords assigned by authors, title words, and any additional access points provided by the IAC. The IAC will also build various kinds of searching aids (e.g., thesauri or synonym tables) to facilitate exploitation of these files. The full text of all communications will be available in digital form so that the system will have its own built-in document delivery capability. There must, however, be algorithms for continuous file reorganization on the basis of "age and activity" factors, so that the communications most likely to be in demand will be in the most accessible storage areas, and the lesser used items will automatically be retired to less accessible storage devices. The data base can be expected to grow with a kind of "snowball" effect, as was true in the IEG experiment, with one communication leading to the creation of others (comments on the original) and these in turn spawning further items.

Notice that the communication network envisaged permits use of the system for both current awareness and retrospective search purposes, and that it is completely paperless. Real-time conversational interaction, terminal to terminal, will also be possible in the system.

The communication network will also include facilities whereby a scientist can build and exploit his own personal information files. His files may consist of references to documents (including network communications), scientific data, or a combination of these, and they may be indexed in any way that the scientist finds convenient. Such files will be "confidential" (i.e., no one else can access them), even though they may contain various documents that are publicly accessible in other ways through the network. The scientist, thus, uses the network facilities to build and exploit his own electronic information files, as well as to access other resources.

The scientist can also use his on-line terminal to access files of data or document references maintained by the IAC, to communicate directly with the staff of the IAC, and to use data bases made accessible to him through the network. These data bases might include the Smithsonian Science Information Exchange data base, or that portion of it that is related to the scope of the IAC, other bibliographic data bases of interest, and a data base on forthcoming conferences and meetings in the field. The network may also provide other types of computer support to the scientist members (e.g., computational and statistical packages).

Within the electronic communications world, a symbiotic relationship between the formal and the informal channels of communication becomes increasingly feasible.

A System Configuration

The configuration of the scientific communication system might resemble the configuration of the intelligence system described earlier. A conceptualization of the overall structure, at a national level, is shown in Figure 15. While this diagram is grossly oversimplified in some respects, it does help to illustrate general principles.

Four levels of processing are identified in the diagram. The Management and Monitoring Level controls the whole operation. It maintains data on all transactions and other activities, volume and distribution of use throughout the system, file characteristics and use factors, and all other data needed for the efficient management of the network. It also handles control of message routing in the network and certain types of billing operations. Besides management and monitoring at the national level, using national computer facilities, there will be monitoring operations conducted at lower levels in the hierarchy, in which regional and local facilities are used.

The Document Access Level, again using national facilities, contains the stores of digital text, various master indexes to these files, and several types of supporting files and resources. The User Support Files contain programs made available for the convenience of all users in the system, including search programs, text editing programs, and programs

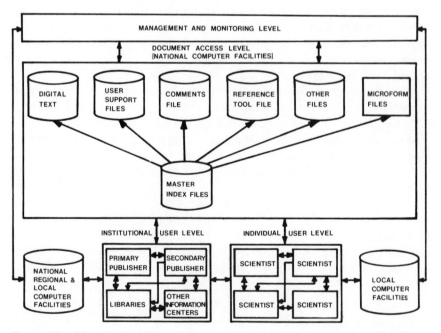

Figure 15. Macrolevel configuration of a national paperless system for scientific and technical communication.

for statistical and mathematical analysis. The Reference Tool File includes various kinds of directories (of data bases, information centers, individuals), providing addresses of resources in the network, dictionaries, and other types of reference tools for the use of authors and others within the system. The Comments File provides a "public record," a kind of mail box, in which any scientist can leave a comment or evaluation relating to any document in the system.

Like the intelligence system, the science communication system is conceived of as storing a document in digital form only once, however many "files" (of primary publishers, secondary publishers, libraries, or individual scientists) it may appear in. Although Figure 15, for convenience, shows the document store as a single central digital file it is necessary that the file be duplicated in various locations to facilitate access and to provide necessary backup. It might also be partitioned so that segments are spread over a number of digital storage facilities. These are important system design considerations but they do not change the overall system conceptualization as illustrated. The digital text files of Figure 15 will contain documents of all kinds: journal articles, technical reports, abstracts, resumés of ongoing research, patents, standards, conference papers and programs, and so on. Everything will be in digital form except, perhaps, for certain kinds of illustrations, which might be stored in some other format, perhaps microform. The Master Index Files contain "public access points" to the text files. What access points are included in these files, and who provides them, need not concern us here. Presumably they will provide access by various types of document numbers and by standard cataloging approaches (author, title, etc.). It seems reasonable too that the primary publisher should have the responsibility for supplying these and any other access points he wishes to provide, unless this role is assumed by the Library of Congress, the British Library, and other organizations that now produce national bibliographies, union catalogs, and similar tools of bibliographic control in printed form.

At the Institutional User Level, there are primary publishers, secondary publishers, libraries, and other information centers. A document, stored once in the digital text files, would exist in the files of one primary publisher, several secondary publishers (indexing and abstracting services), and many libraries and other information centers, as well as the files of individual scientists and other users. "Existing in the files of" an institution or an individual may mean only that these institutions or individuals include various pointers to the document in their own access files. The primary publisher will provide access points corresponding to the present divisions or "packages" in scientific publishing. Thus a society may still publish a number of "journals," and various items in the digital files will be designated as belonging to these various journals. The primary publisher will also provide access to the document by author, title, and, perhaps, some form of subject indexing.

The access points given to a document by the secondary publishers will correspond to the index terms or other subject codes now contained in the published indexing and abstracting services. Where an abstract is created for a document by a secondary service (as opposed to being supplied by author or publisher), this will be stored as digital text in a separate file at the Document Access Level. Increasingly, however, the responsibility for preparation of abstracts will pass to the primary publisher, and an "official" abstract, prepared according to national or international standards, will be stored as part of the text of the document itself. Although an article may exist in the data bases of 20 secondary services, then, it will be abstracted and descriptively cataloged only once, although it will be indexed in 20 different ways to represent differing emphases and viewpoints. Likewise, libraries, other information centers, and individual scientists may include a document in their files by providing their own pointers to it.

As shown in Figure 15, computer facilities will be national, regional, and local. The overall management functions, the document access functions, and, possibly, some of the institutional access functions will be handled by national computer facilities. Other functions will be handled by local and regional facilities. At the Individual User Level, a scientist's own files, consisting of his pointers to the digital text files and whatever else he wishes to include there (correspondence, comments, notes, drafts) will be stored on a local facility, perhaps a minicomputer, whereas institutional files will be handled by local or regional computing resources.

All of these computer facilities—national, regional, and local—must be integrated within the overall network so that there is free communication among all levels of the hierarchy as well as within each level: scientist to scientist, scientist to institution, institution to scientist, institution to institution, and all of these with the national stores. The scientist may go directly to the document stores under certain circumstances or he can obtain access through primary publishers, secondary publishers, libraries, or other information centers. These various institutions can disseminate among each other and down to the individual user. Individual users can also exchange materials among themselves.

Two further points about the system should be noted. First, Figure 15 depicts a system at a national level, but the eventual system will actually be an international system composed of a group of interlinked national systems, rather than one of only national scope. Second, the system is intended to provide for electronic access to all types of documents read for their information value but is not intended to replace print on paper for items read solely for recreational purposes. *Playboy*, for example, is unlikely to be enhanced by soft copy display.

7

Feasibility and Benefits
of the Electronic System

The scenario presented in the last chapter is by no means farfetched. Everything described is technologically possible in 1978, and the economic feasibility is likely to improve considerably in the next decade and beyond. Senders *et al.* (1975), in discussing the feasibility of an electronic journal, have claimed that it "... is easily realisable with equipment that can be bought off the shelf today, at a price which compares favourably with the costs of paper publication [p. 46]." Clayton and Nisenoff (1976), after completing a rather ambitious forecast of technology for the scientific and technical information communities, conclude: "Hardware technology is not a limiting factor to any electronic implementation of an S & T information communication system over the next 25 years [p. 167]." Bell (1977), too, has pointed out that "The substitution of electronic delivery for paper is not primarily a question of technology, but of costs [p. 13]."

Implementation of the system will require various levels of access, in the same way that the intelligence system requires various levels of access. Some of these levels will involve the use of mass storage devices that are less expensive than present disk storage yet give rapid access capabilities. A number of efficient storage devices are now commercially available and considerable improvements can be expected in the near future. Senders *et al.* (1975) point out that "Mass storage has increased in capacity since the days of Bush and Licklider to the point where an electronic journal is no longer constrained by storage capacities [p. 73]." The system also implies the existence of a huge network of mainframe computers and of minicomputers all capable of communicating with each other and of transferring data from one part of the network to another. A worldwide network of this kind does not yet exist, although elements of it do, and more efficient and less costly modes of data transfer will be needed to implement such a network. The problems of implementing a global system, however, seem more political than technological. Finally, the system envisioned requires an exponential increase in the number of available terminal devices and, presumably, the capability of producing such devices at a cost considerably below present costs. All of these developments are very likely to occur before the year 2000, and various technological forecasts, including those summarized by Anderla (1973), suggest that the scientific communication system described is technologically feasible now and will be economically advantageous long before the year 2000. It is sobering to remember that 25 years ago there were no computer applications in publishing, in information retrieval, or in any of the activities previously mentioned, that the first machine-readable bibliographic data base was still almost 15 years off, and that interplanetary flight remained in the realms of science fiction.

We are already a great deal closer to implementing a paperless system than many might suppose. At least, various elements of the system already exist in experimental, prototype, or operational form, and several of the capabilities have already been demonstrated. It is appropriate, then, to consider what elements do exist and what some of our present achievements are. Recent or ongoing activities that will contribute toward achieving the electronic information system include the following:

1. The increasing use of machine-readable input in the production of primary and secondary publications.
2. The rapid growth, over the past decade, in the availability of machine-readable files of bibliographic and other forms of data, and the equally rapid growth of information services derived from these data bases.
3. The development and growth of on-line, time-shared, interactive computer systems, and the application of these to information services.

4. The emergence of networks of connecting computers, and continued work on the development of improved telecommunications capabilities by satellite and other means. Improved digital transmission capabilities are particularly important to the implementation of a worldwide system for science communication.

5. The use of on-line systems for indexing and cataloging operations and for cooperative enterprises within the library world. The most important of these is the cooperative cataloging system developed by the Ohio College Library Center, as described by Kilgour *et al.* (1972).

6. The use of on-line systems in several universities to support the building and exploitation of information files by individual scientists and other professionals.

7. The development of international communication systems, using on-line facilities, by various business enterprises.

8. The increasing use of computer-aided instruction (CAI) throughout the educational process, and the development of systems, such as PLATO, of increasing size and sophistication (see Bitzer and Skaperdas, 1972).

9. The emergence of cable television and of the use of this communications medium in interactive applications, as exemplified by the work of the Mitre Corporation (see, for example, Stetten, 1971a,b; Volk, 1971).

10. The growth of interest in the development of "information utilities," as described in Sackman and Nie (1970).

11. The conceptualization of a more widespread application of computer technology to scientific publishing, as exemplified by the work on the economic and technical feasibility of Editorial Processing Centers.

12. The development of more efficient and economical mass storage devices, as exemplified by the use of laser, magnetic domain, and charge-coupled devices.

13. The development of improved and innovative display devices such as the plasma panel and its modification, the touch panel (see Stifle, 1971).

14. The routine use of digital communications by press services and other disseminators of news, and the use of video terminals in the writing and editorial functions of newspapers.

15. The wide availability and increasing use of programs for on-line text editing.

16. The conceptualization of parallel developments in other sectors of society, one example of which is the "automated office" as discussed by Yasaki (1975).
17. Recent experience in "computer conferencing" as described by Price (1975).
18. Experience with the use of large text files (100 million words or more) in the legal retrieval field.
19. The clear demonstration of the technical feasibility of a completely paperless communication system within the intelligence community, as described earlier in this book.

This list is intended to be illustrative rather than complete, and it is not presented in any logical order. In fact, the last item may be the most significant.

The implementation of the system will involve the coming together, or rather the deliberate "putting together" of a number of separate services, activities, and experiments now in existence. It is significant to note that a rather sophisticated on-line system, employing minicomputers, and having many of the capabilities needed to implement a paperless system of the type described, is already commercially available in Sweden (Leimdörfer, 1975). The "Minicomputer News Monitor," designed to facilitate the distribution and exploitation of general and financial news released by international wire services, includes the following capabilities:

1. Ability to search large bodies of text of current news from an on-line terminal
2. Ability to alert users to important developments in the news by terminal display of words in current news messages that have above-normal rates of occurrence
3. Ability to alert users to current news items that match their stored interest profiles
4. Ability to convert search terms from one language to another
5. Ability to allow users to superimpose their own additions on the incoming flow of news items

The electronic system described is unlikely to cause any diminution in the amount of material published. In fact, the reverse is more likely to be true. The economics of electronic publishing will be less dependent on how much is published than is true of the conventional print-on-paper medium. Consequently, there will be less need to reject a communication for economic reasons rather than on the basis of scientific merit. Folk (1977) suggests that an electronic system:

would have at least as much garbage in it as libraries do today—probably more—but the garbage would not clog the system. Computer-based indexing would guide a new breed of scholars to the literature, and users could retrieve everything bearing on a subject they wish to investigate deeply, or skim the cream by requesting only widely cited and reviewed articles. Inaccurate, slovenly, and plagiarized articles would be panned; at last it would be possible for authors to publish and perish at the same time [p. 79].

More importantly, the paperless system should significantly reduce delays in all aspects of the dissemination cycle. The composition process itself should be speeded up and so should the whole interaction among writers, publishers, and referees. Papers will get into primary data bases more quickly than they do at present, and significant improvements will occur in the time it takes for papers to reach secondary publishers, to be indexed and abstracted, to be disseminated to the user community, to be assimilated by this community, and to be available for retrospective searching. The potential for economies of time in the composition and recording functions (i.e., prepublication activities) alone is considerable. King *et al.* (1976), for example, present data to show that, on the average, the author of a paper in the life sciences spends 81.6 hours of his own time in preparing the initial manuscript, and that this is accompanied by an average of 36 hours of "support time." When manuscript revisions have to be made, the time expenditure, of course, goes up. The data indicate that over 60% of all papers in the life sciences require at least one revision. When revision is taken into account, an author in the life sciences spends an average of 96.6 hours of his own time on each paper, and this is accompanied by an average of 47.5 hours of support time. All of these time expenditures, as well as elapsed times, can be considerably reduced in the electronic world through the benefits of text editing and correction capabilities, and by the elimination of duplication in keyboarding activities.

On-line text editing capabilities offer considerable advantages to the scientist as writer and to the editor of science materials. A very useful review of the subject is given by Van Dam and Rice (1971), and video editing is also discussed by Carlson (1973). Carlson quotes Van Dam on the advantages to the writer of FRESS (File Retrieval and Editing System):

The second mode makes FRESS unique and allows the writer-author-composer, if he is at all comfortable with a keyboard, to browse through his files looking for relevant materials, to cull from this data base, to "cut and paste" the fragments together, and to try out different combinations and phrasings of ideas and always be able to have clean copy in front of him in seconds.

In short, it allows him to get his thinking work done faster and better than with pencil and paper. Furthermore, since he works on-line he need not leave his manuscript for continuous cycles of secretarial transcription followed by proofreading two days later of what has been done. At this point FRESS becomes more than a mechanical aid for typographical correction; it becomes a thinking tool, an intelligence amplifier [p. 117].

A specific example of some of the input procedures that might be involved in electronic publication has been provided by Thompson (1976):

> To take a specific example of how this works in practice, the original of the text you are reading was prepared on the BNR computer system via a terminal in one BNR location, using a rather fine text editing program that makes a two-finger hunt-and-pecker feel like a 60-words-a-minute typist. Errors are easily corrected, and subsequent retypings are performed by a high-speed computer printer. The process never adds errors, only steadily removes them. No more retyping errors!
>
> When the paper was in its formative stage, it was transferred to the editor of *Telesis* in another company location by issuing a very simple command to the computer. Instantly, the text was transferred to his computer files. He then obtained a printed version from a computer printer at his location and read the paper at his leisure. His comments led to changes being made, via his terminal, to the version on his files. The revised version was then sent back to me, and so on through several iterations. However, a request for a more technical version was received from this publication, this time outside the company. The original work now split into two distinctly different papers, whose character diverged as each was repeatedly revised. The second version, which had to be mailed because no electronic link existed, took several weeks to reach that editor, because of problems in the mail system. Meanwhile, the first version continued to be exchanged electronically. How much easier it would have been with a data network to link with that second editor's computer system, through "intelligent" interfaces! The second text could have been sent by wire, in machine readable form, ready for immediate entry into his modern publishing plant, which has its own computer typesetting system [p. 114].

It should be noted that this description still visualizes that the final publication will be typeset by computer and issued in printed form. This should be regarded as merely an interim stage in the development of a system in which distribution of "papers," as well as their preparation, will be handled through data networks.

Another account of the current capabilities of text editors is given by Folk (1977). The system described is TROFF, developed by Bell Laboratories, and used to compose in-house reports as well as a technical newsletter:

> This system has several major advantages and represents the current state of the art: (1) it runs on inexpensive computer hardware, (2) it is usable by persons

with little training, and (3) it uses an inexpensive phototypesetter. TROFF runs on the UNIX time sharing system developed by Bell Laboratories as a general operating system for the Digital Equipment Corporation PDP 11/45 and 11/70 computers. UNIX includes a powerful context editor that allows a typist to input text at either an on-line terminal or an off-line cassette terminal. The typist inputs equations and tables using special programs that can be learned in a few hours. Once in the computer, the draft can be corrected by using special commands, such as *spell,* which looks up every word in an on-line dictionary and produces a list of words not in the dictionary, and *typo,* which uses the rules of English spelling (such as they are) to find possible typographical errors. Other programs have been written by various users to help authors improve their style. A word-frequency command provides a list of words used in a document and a count of how many times each was used. Another program prints the lines in which some troublesome homophones (such as *there/their*) or pet words (such as *obviously* and *clearly*) occur so that a writer can avoid error.

The UNIX typist then inserts commands to provide for centering, underlining, footnoting, equations, tables, indentation and other typographical specifications. The TROFF program then processes the file with text and interspersed command language and produces a decent-looking, justified typescript [pp. 75–76].

Dissemination and assimilation of scientific information should also be speeded up by virtue of the fact that indexes to ongoing research and to the technical report literature should be more visible to the community at large because they will be more accessible. Informal communication can be more effective and more rapid in the electronic system because a scientist can transmit materials to other scientists more easily and will be able to interact in "real time" with colleagues thousands of miles away. Senders *et al.* (1975) have also pointed out that cooperative authorship, especially international cooperative authorship, will be greatly facilitated.

Some of the advantages of using the computer in informal communication have been summarized by Price (1975) as follows:

The use of the computer for conferencing makes the computer a true communications medium, supplementing its use as a medium for storage and computation. Because of the features of storage, retrieval, and data processing, not available through other media, computer conferencing is a significant advance over other communications media [p. 499].

As teleconferencing is more widely considered and tried, it can emerge as not only a second-best alternative to "being there" but as a positive advantage in many kinds of information-sharing, problem-solving, and managerial processes [p. 510].

Computer conferencing opens up the possibility for researchers and policymakers of an electronic newsletter-like service, one which would be much more interactive and information-rich than the printed version. The newsletter "subscribers" would constitute a permanent conference of variable membership; each conferee could receive messages sent to all members, additional news or greater detail in an augmented service, or answers to queries—electronic letters-to-the-editor. Such a system would be particularly useful for integrated complementary research programs at a variety of locations, or tying together special-interest subgroups within professional and technical societies |p. 511|.

And finally:

It would seem that computer conferencing has the potential of becoming a communication/problem solving medium that offers a believable way to directly challenge the current rapid drift toward an impasse caused by too much information, too little time to process it, and too little capability within human beings alone to interrelate and evaluate information even if processed |p. 514|.[1]

Computer conferencing systems already exist and the number of users of such systems is steadily increasing. A notable example is the Electronic Information Exchange System, operated by the New Jersey Institute of Technology. This system contains four components considered essential to an efficient electronic exchange environment:

NOTEBOOK   Personal space to allow an individual to write, using editing capabilities supplied by the system.

MESSAGE   The ability of one individual to transmit any type of message, in private, to any other individual in the network.

CONFERENCE   "Common space" to allow a group with shared interests to communicate, a message entered being accessible to all members of the group.

BULLETIN   Public space to permit messages to be entered and made accessible, without restriction, to all users of the system.

It is clear that a system of this kind already goes a long way toward providing the capabilities needed for the type of electronic system conceptualized in the preceeding chapter. It would be a simple matter to create and issue an electronic journal within this environment.

Because the full text of documents will be rapidly accessible from digital stores, one of the most serious weaknesses in the present system—the document delivery function—will be considerably improved. At present we have reached a somewhat anomalous situation in which references to documents can be found, through on-line search, in a matter of minutes, but it may take some days or even weeks to obtain the documents themselves through conventional purchase or interlibrary loan procedures.

---

[1] Reproduced from *The Delphi Method*, 1975 written by Harold A. Linstone and Murray Turoff with permission of publishers, Addison-Wesley, Advanced Book Program, Reading, Massachusetts.

Perhaps the major benefit of the electronic system, however, is that it makes the universe of information resources more widely accessible than ever before. Any scientist who has access to a terminal has access to this universe of resources. The scientist at a remote location, who is now at a disadvantage in terms of rapid access to information resources, will be on equal terms with the scientist at a major university, or research center, supporting a great research library. Geographic boundaries will no longer be a barrier to effective scientific communication, and remote data bases in other countries will be as accessible as those in the scientist's own institution. Moreover, if all science documents are equally accessible, and if the division into journal "packages" essentially disappears, the present problems caused by the fragmentation and dispersion of the literature of a field will also disappear. Parker (1975) summarizes the advantages thus:

> Computer information retrieval systems can make it possible for any citizen to have access to stored information without expensive labor costs of access. Specific items of information being sought could be made accessible on demand without sorting through libraries full of paper [p. 104].

Folk (1977) foresees great benefits to science:

> The widespread adoption of electronic publishing will herald an important new day in science. The act of publication will become the first step in scientific communication, rather than the last step, as it is too often today. The scientific literature will become unified, reversing the recent trend toward diverse forms of publication. Scientists everywhere will have equal access to the scientific literature, so that the advantages of being in a famous center of research will be substantially lessened. Scientists in obscure universities or poor countries will be able to participate in scientific discourse more readily [p. 80].

Some Cost Considerations

Some cost considerations relating to the electronic journal have been discussed by Roistacher (1978), Senders et al (1975), Senders (1976, 1977), and Folk (1977). Drawing upon experience with on-line composition at the Center for Advanced Computation, University of Illinois, Roistacher concludes that a paper of 15 pages could be written in about 22.5 hours of connnect time. At computer costs of $2 per hour and communication costs of $3 per hour, the paper could be composed for a total cost of around $110 to $120, about $7.50 per published page. At off-line night rates, however, these costs could be even lower: $1.60 per hour for computer services and $2 per hour for communication, for a total cost of $81, or $5.40 per published page. He contrasts this with the present composition costs for technical journals which he claims are in the range of $25 to $28 per page and which will obviously go much higher.

It must be noted that Roistacher's estimates for the number of hours needed to compose a paper are well below those provided by King *et al.* (1976), as presented earlier in the chapter. King's figure of around 80 hours per paper, however, must include a considerable amount of "think" time which would not necessarily involve the use of on-line resources. Even if we multiply Roistacher's figures by four, we have a situation in which the electronic composition is at least economically competitive with the conventional composition. The costs of the latter can only get worse. The costs of the former are quite likely to improve. Roistacher goes on to point out that, for a journal publishing 300 papers a year, with an average length of 15 pages (i.e., 4500 printed pages), storage in direct access files could cost as little as $2200 a year. He estimates computer support for editorial processing of this journal to be no more than $5000 per year.

Folk (1977) contrasts central storage costs for maintenance of an electronic journal with the distributed storage costs associated with maintaining printed journals on library shelves:

> Suppose one printed volume of a journal costs $25 and is purchased and shelved by 100 libraries at a total cost of $2,500. Storing 100 volumes requires about ten square feet of library floor space or, at current construction costs, about $400. Thus, the capital cost of the volume to the library system is $2,900. A volume is about 5 megabytes (MB), or 1,000 pages of 5,000 bytes (or characters) each. An AED controller and disc system for 536 MB (formatted) costs about $75,000. This system would hold 100 different journals for a cost of $750 per journal. Mass storage devices with much cheaper costs (less than $1/MB) are commercially available, but for a distributed system using minicomputers, a single system will not exceed a few hundred megabytes [p. 81].

This cost analysis is very modest, both in terms of subscription costs and in number of libraries considered. It is clear that the economics of storage greatly favor the electronic journal as either subscription cost or the number of libraries providing access to a particular title are increased.

As far as transmission costs are concerned, Roistacher estimates that a user could access any part of an electronic journal (contents page, abstracts, or full text) at a cost of about $1.80 per hour plus $3 per hour in network costs. In non-prime time these costs could be reduced to as little as $3 per hour for computation and communication. An article of 15 pages could be printed out on a 30 character-per-second (cps) terminal at a total prime time cost of about $1.90 or non-prime time cost of about $1.40. It could be printed off-line on a line printer for about 20 cents. In this case, costs of handling and mailing must be added.[2]

Folk (1977) quotes a figure of $1 to $5, depending on the location of the user in relation to the data base, and on time of day, for printing a 10-page, 50,000 byte article on a 30 cps terminal. He points out that this is inexpensive when contrasted with the cost of an interlibrary loan, which he estimates to be about $7 to $8.

In a realistic cost–benefit comparison, the electronic system might already outperform present operations. Senders *et al.* (1975) have undertaken a more complete economic analysis of the "electronic journal." They calculate that the full text of about 25,000 science journals (i.e., about half of the present world output, according to best available estimates) would require 4×10^{12} bits of on-line storage each year. If laser memories are used, they calculate that this will cost some $1.2 million a year, which is a very small amount considering the quantity of text involved. Taking only journal production costs into account, they estimate that the cost of the electronic journal would be equal to the cost of the paper journal by 1978. When all "hidden costs" are considered, however, including costs of disseminating to terminals and use by scientists on-line, the cost of the electronic journal will equal the cost of the paper journal by about 1996 and will be cheaper thereafter.

Senders (1977) has discussed capital and other costs in the following terms:

> For an initial investment of approximately £100,000,000 this year, we could effectively substitute an electronic system which would be almost identical in cost to the present paper publishing systems. The capital costs would be spread over 5 years. The actual cost in the first year would be close to £7 or £800,000,000, which is a very small figure in comparison to the overall actual cost of distributing the world's scientific literature. If we try to make electronic a small journal of about 900 pages per year with no more than 2,500 subscribers, both private and institutional, the economics of the situation indicate a crossover point in the middle or late 1990s. However, if we set up a system to handle the entire body of English language scientific publications at once, the crossover point has already been passed. This is true even though we assume an enormous initial investment for the supplying of terminals to scientists in sufficient numbers to ensure that access can be had by all.
>
> None of the above cost figures take into account the value of saving time. The delay in publication implicit in the electronic system is the editorial processing time, which runs about six weeks for most of the North American journals. The

---

[2] In a personal communication, Roistacher has since indicated that the computer costs quoted (but not the communications costs) have all been reduced by about 20%.

average lag in publication for the North American journals is about one year, and in certain of the social sciences and humanities, as much as two years. No one seems to be able to equate dollar savings with time savings, but there seems to be some correspondence. This would suggest that the crossover points actually occurred some time ago. My original estimate of the crossover for the North American corpus of scientific information, based on a comprehensive model of costs, was around 1971 [pp. 6-7].

This cost analysis appears somewhat pessimistic in some respects. First, it assumes that the journal will bear the full cost of the telecommunications network, including terminal costs. This is unrealistic because the overall network is likely to exist for other reasons, as the scientists will use terminals for many different purposes. Moreover, all of the potential savings, in writing and recording time, in communication among authors, publishers, and referees, and in dissemination and use costs, are not taken into account. If the present science communication system is realistically costed, it represents very considerable expenditures indeed. King *et al.* (1976), for example, come up with an estimate of over 12 billion dollars as the total annual cost of disseminating scientific and technical information in the United States by present procedures, and the electronic system has the potential for offering considerable savings in a number of the total functions involved. There are many hidden costs in the present system and some of these costs are easily overlooked. Parker (1975) has something very pertinent to say about one aspect of these hidden costs:

> Before the industrial revolution many "industries" were cottage industries with people working in their own homes. In an information age it may be desirable to partially return to a style of work at home for many information occupations. When computer terminals and computer networks are as accessible to every home as telephones and the cost of word processing on computer terminals with electronic storage is cheaper than word processing on typewriters with paper storage, then many people in word processing occupations will work from home the way many computer programmers in the United States now work from home using portable computer terminals and telephone connections [pp. 106-107].

Parker goes on to point out that the situation in which more work is done at home, and less commuting is involved, offers the possibility of considerable savings in money, time, and natural resources (e.g., gasoline). These are all examples of hidden costs that must be taken into account in any complete and realistic cost comparison between the print-on-paper and the paperless system.

Price (1975, p. 509) quotes Turoff (1973) on the economic advantages of the electronic processing environment:

> The forthcoming wide introduction of digital data networks will probably provide computerized conferencing systems with another order of magnitude edge in costs when compared to conventional verbal telephone conference calls. Thus, economic pressure may force the various (technical) problems (of computer conferencing) to be resolved favorably, so that computerized conferencing becomes a major application on such networks. The anticipated future reduction of costs, by the late seventies, for computer terminals with CRT, perhaps placing them in the same purchase range as home color TV receivers, suggests a picture of future society in which a major substitution of communications for transportation can take place.

The question of the feasibility of increasing use of communications to replace inter-city and intra-city travel has been addressed by a number of other writers. Day (1973), for example, has pointed out the need to examine this substitutability issue from more than a strictly cost–benefit viewpoint. Other important considerations include the behavioral factors determining why people choose to travel and the secondary environmental costs associated with the two alternatives.

Price (1975) has indicated that the present cost of transmitting business correspondence through an on-line network can be as little as 25 to 50 cents per message. This is considerably cheaper than long distance telephone costs and competitive with mail service, over which it has many obvious advantages. An added saving comes from the fact that the same message can be sent to many destinations with no significant increases in costs. If the value of the time of participants and if travel costs are taken into account, dramatic savings are possible when computer conferencing is used in place of face-to-face encounter.

By 1977 a number of major corporations in the United States were moving toward the implementation of "electronic mail systems." Combustion Engineering, for example, has implemented a system called ATOM (Automatic Transmission of Mail). ATOM gives each participant a secure electronic "mailbox" which stores all mail and messages sent to or from the participant. The user can scan, read, print, forward with notations, "pend," or create mail and messages to or from any location in the world. The system is designed to be used by managers and their secretaries, with no special knowledge of data processing required.

It is perhaps worth nothing here that the possibility of a computer conferencing system handling many communications now commonly handled by business correspondence is quite different from the concept of an "electronic mail handling system" as proposed to the United States

Postal Service by Arthur D. Little, Inc. (1974). In this approach to mail handling "electronically," mail is accepted either as paper or as micro-form, converted to machine-readable form, transmitted to receiving points electronically, sorted, and reconverted to paper for actual delivery. In this type of system only the transmission is "electronic."

As in the intelligence environment, it is the benefits of the electronic system, as discussed, rather than potential cost savings, by which a move to paperless processing can most easily be justified. Parker (1975) has gone far beyond most other writers in his claims regarding the eco-nomic and social significance of improved information processing. He points out that we are on the brink of a new social revolution—the information revolution—which will be just as important as the industrial revolution. This implies a transition from an industrial society to an information processing society, a society in which information processing will dominate industrial production as a labor activity. He goes on to predict that future economic gains will be made through the information sector rather than the production sector, and that governments in the long run have more to gain from investment in improved information processing than from further investment in industrial productivity. Finally, Parker makes a strong recommendation that now is the time for govern-ments to develop the communication systems needed to achieve these economic gains:

> It makes a great difference to the economic development of a country whether a communication network (or new nodes on the network) is treated as essential infrastructure needed for development or whether it is treated as a consumption or luxury item to be provided only after the demand is great [p. 113].

In Chapter 5 certain data relating to the duplication of research effort were presented. These data suggest that very considerable savings (in the range of hundreds of millions of dollars) could result if the electronic system leads to the dissemination of research results more rapidly, com-pletely, and effectively throughout the science community.

Any prediction of a full-scale implementation of an electronic system, to replace the existing scientific communication system, can be considered to rest on the following assumptions:

1. That costs of computer processing and of telecommunications will continue to decline relative to manual processing and the use of other means of communication
2. That hardware, particularly terminals, will become increasingly accessible

Let us examine these assumptions a little further. We have already witnessed a quite dramatic decline in the cost of telecommunications in support of on-line systems. When on-line retrieval systems for instructional purposes were first demonstrated at the University of Illinois in 1970, estimated computer costs for 1 hour of demonstration were in the range of $3 to $5. But the communications costs, using a conventional telephone connection from Urbana to Santa Monica, were estimated to be about $30 for one hour of demonstration. Today, through TELENET, the same demonstration can be conducted at a communication cost of $3 per hour. Roistacher (1978) claims that "Computer communication costs have been calculated as declining by 15%/year since about 1960, a trend which is expected to continue into the 1980s [p. 5]."

A complete technological forecast of developments in the communication of scientific and technical information has been prepared for the National Science Foundation by Forecasting International, Inc. This study, reported by Clayton and Nisenoff (1976), includes forecasts that are very encouraging to the concept of a paperless system. Some of the major predictions of this study, covering cost, efficiency, and availability factors, are given in Table 7. Data collected suggest that by the year 1990 as much as 40% of all scientific and technical publications may be composed on-line, as much as 75% of the output of scientific and technical publications will be transmitted from author to user by electronic means, as much as 82% of all scientific and technical information will exist in machine-readable form, and as much as 92% of the population of generators and users of scientific and technical information will have access to on-line terminals. The purchase price of a central processing "unit" is projected to decline from $108,000 in 1980 to $6000 in 1990, while performance in this period may increase from 9 million instructions per second to 100 million instructions per second.

Clayton and Nisenoff also point out that the number of terminals that can be associated with a single central processor is increasing rapidly and that new technology, not yet identified, may well reduce various aspects of costs and improve various levels of performance even further. In short, the costs of the electronic system will continue to decline into the foreseeable future—but the costs of conventional communication systems in science can only continue to escalate. Folk (1977) summarizes the situation as follows:

> Current costs of preparing a machine-readable text, storing it on a computer, communicating with the remote computer, and computer time for the user to read or print the document are low enough that, for many applications in scientific pub-

TABLE 7

General Characteristics of Future S&T Telecomputing Communications Systems[a]

Parameter	Value		
	1980	1985	1990
Number of computers in U.S.			
a. Mainframes	55K	70K	90K
b. Minicomputers	300K	650K	1.25M
c. Microprocessors	12M	50M	100M
Mainframe computers			
a. Cost/performance ($/MIP)	15,000	500	10
b. Performance (MIPS/SEC)	9	30	100
c. Add time (NS)	12	5	2
d. Multiply time (NS)	110	50	20
e. Maximum number of terminals/ computer	275	1300	8000
Main memory			
a. Minimum capacity (10^6 bits)	10	20	80
b. Maximum capacity (10^6 bits)	120	300	1500
c. Cost/bit (¢)	4	2	1
d. Memory cycle time (NS)	30	10	2
Minicomputers—cost performance of 8k unit (10^6 bits/sec/$)	0.3	4.0	50
Performance of magnetic tape			
a. Average access (sec)	9	5	3.5
b. Cost (¢/bit)	6×10^{-4}	3×10^{-4}	1.5×10^{-4}
c. Packing density (bits/in.^{2})	0.3×10^6	0.6×10^6	1.5×10^6
Performance of disk RAM storage			
a. Average access (MS)	10	5	2.5
b. Cost of moving head (¢/bit)	2×10^{-3}	1×10^{-3}	5×10^{-4}
c. Cost of fixed head (¢/bit)	15×10^{-3}	6×10^{-3}	3×10^{-3}
d. Packing density (bits/in.^{2})	5×10^6	15×10^6	50×10^6
Cost of semiconductor RAM storage (¢/bit)	4×10^{-4}	2×10^{-4}	1.5×10^{-4}
Maximum RAM capacity per computer (bits)	10^9	10^{10}	10^{11}
High speed printer performance (K char/sec)	600	2100	7500
Terminals			
a. Cost of intelligent units ($)	1900	1400	1300
b. Cost of TTY type units ($)	600	400	325
c. Total number in U.S. (M)	4	12	30
Communications			
a. Number of telephones in the U.S. (M)	160	190	220
b. Cost of a phone line ($/hr)	9.0	7.5	6.0
c. Cost of a satellite channel ($/ch/yr)	150	50	20
Software			
a. Cost per line of code ($)	7.0	5.0	3.0
b. Ratio, software to hardware	80/20	85/15	87/13
Logic circuits			
a. Cost per unit (¢)	40	20	15
b. Packing density (circuits/cm^3)	2000	5000	40,000

[a] From Clayton and Nisenoff (1976) by permission of Forecasting International, Ltd.

lishing, a computer-based system may be less expensive than the existing paper-and-ink system. Rapidly decreasing computer and communications costs indicate that electronic publication will be increasingly cost-effective compared to alternative systems [p. 72].

There seems little doubt that a paperless information system of the type described is technologically feasible now at a national if not an international level. This is not to imply that no technological problems exist. Many do. But they are problems relating to the identification of most practical or economic approaches rather than problems of feasibility of implementation. Moreover, technological feasibility does not automatically imply the practicality of implementation when economic, social, and psychological factors are all considered. The next chapter will present some problems that need to be solved before the paperless system can move from conceptualization to realization.

8

Problems of Implementation

It has already been claimed that the paperless communication system can be implemented now. By this is meant that there exist no real technological barriers to its implementation. This is not to imply, however, that there are no problems to be solved before the conversion to an electronic system can be accomplished. Many problems will need solving before the completely electronic communication system comes into being. These seem to be of three major types:

1. Technological
2. Intellectual
3. Social and psychological

which is a sequence of increasing complexity.

Technological Problems

Technological problems do exist. But they are problems of scale rather than scientific or technological breakthrough. Although I have spoken of an "electronic system," it is clear that I am in fact speaking of a very large number of separate systems. The system design problems involved in linking these into a cohesive network, so that one system can freely exchange data with another, are very considerable ones. Moreover, there are many complex problems of file organization, and file interconnection, that would need to be solved. In theory, a particular bibliographic record (e.g., the full text of a paper) need only be stored once in a universal system. Although this record might exist in hundreds of different files, these files might simply store "pointers" to the complete record. In practice, there are many problems involved in implementing such a "one record" system, when questions of reliability and backup, and problems of queuing, are taken into account.

Another type of technological problem was mentioned earlier. An electronic information system of the scale suggested in the scenario implies the development and implementation, on an international scale, of efficient and inexpensive networks for the transmission of digital data, without the need for digital-to-analog and analog-to-digital conversion. As Parker (1975) has pointed out, the time-shared digital network must also have redundant channels and error-checking procedures. Such networks do not presently exist, although there is every hope that they will exist in the near future.

Telecommunications costs for data processing applications continue to decline. The Telenet Communications Corporation, for example, in a newsletter of September 1976 (*The Telenet Report*), announced the expansion of their teleprocessing network from the United States to Canada, Mexico, and the United Kingdom. Transatlantic connections were expected to range from $8 to $15 per hour. The company suggests that "talking to a computer overseas may cost as little as 15 to 25 cents a minute in the not too distant future."

Senders *et al.* (1975) estimated that the implementation of a dedicated communication network needed to support an electronic journal would require a capital expenditure of about $5 million and operating expenses of about $5 million a year. If the capital expenditure is amortized over 20 years, the cost of using the network, at an estimated rate of 150,000 hours a month, could work out to as little as 70 cents per connect hour.

At the technological level, there are also problems of reliability and security. An electronic information system of the type proposed must have an extremely high level of reliability and of redundancy. All files need to be "backed up" so that there is no possibility of complete loss. Computers in the network need to be interchangeable so that an overload in demand can be switched to another unit having processing time available. Surplus computing power must be available so that a spare unit can be plugged in to replace one that is malfunctioning. A

breakdown at any part of the network may lead to temporary degrada-
tion of performance (e.g., as measured in response time) but it cannot be
allowed to interrupt a particular facet of service completely. Problems of
file security also have to be tackled because not all files will be accessible to everyone. The personal files that a scientist builds himself, for
example, should be accessible only to him or to other individuals that he
has specifically authorized to use them. Depending upon the methods of
file organization employed, the security of a particular file may be a
question of securing sets of access points so that a particular individual
can retrieve a particular record only through a certain set of access
points (e.g., those he has himself provided) and not through the many
other sets of access points that are open only to other individuals or
institutions.

Other requirements imposed include the capacity for accommodating
the very large character set that will be needed in a multidisciplinary
system of this kind (see Rule, 1975), and possible needs for data
compression to economize on digital storage costs (see Heaps, 1975).

Another problem is that presented by graphic material. The transmission and display of high-quality graphic material may require an interface between digital and microfiche storage until some newer technology
(e.g., videodisk) makes some alternative method economically feasible.
Roistacher (1978) discusses the graphics problem in the following
terms:

> Problems involving the handling of graphics will require special efforts by the
> sponsors of virtual journals. Tabular data and graphs involve no special problems
> since they are within the printing and plotting capabilities of available terminals.
> However, while there is a standard method for representing character data in com-
> puter files, graphic information is presently represented in nonstandard, device-
> specific formats. A generally readable virtual journal will require a standard code
> for storing graphics, so that any terminal with a plotting capability will be able to
> print both the text and the graphics of an article.
>
> The storage and transmission of photographs and colored graphics are beyond
> the capabilities of any equipment that will be generally available in the next few
> years. Such materials will have to be distributed by mail, either by the author or by
> the journal [p. 6].

Finally, at the technological level, there are the problems of designing
and implementing a giant management information system for monitoring purposes or, more likely, a whole set of such systems. Extremely
sophisticated monitoring systems will be needed for purposes of efficient
message routing, for maintaining statistics on file size and traffic, for billing purposes, and for a whole host of management control activities. An
excellent discussion of the requirements for monitoring an on-line
information system is given by Mittman and Dominick (1973).

Intellectual Problems

Some of the intellectual problems that must be faced are due to the following facts:

1. A number of different query languages may have to be used in switching among data bases.
2. Different data bases are likely to involve the use of different vocabularies (thesauri, lists of subject headings, classification schemes, or simple lists of keywords), and the characteristics of these vocabularies must be learned before the data bases can be used at a high level of effectiveness.
3. Different (natural) languages may be involved.
4. The on-line user may be faced with such a wealth of potentially relevant resources that he will not know which file is most likely to satisfy his current information need. Under the worst of conditions, he may not locate the file that is most relevant to his need. Under somewhat better circumstances, he may locate the file but only after he has spent considerable time and effort trying other, less productive sources.

Some of these problems, if not exactly solved at the present time, have at least been recognized. The need for a common language of interrogation (query language or command language) has been addressed in some detail by Landau (1976):

> In the early '70's it was hoped by many in the field that the various system operators would agree upon reasonably similar commands for the various required functions. This fond hope has not been realized and there is a steady proliferation of unique sets of commands being developed in a number of systems, not only in the field of STI but many other fields such as logistics, personnel, finance, management, etc. Numerous experts have, through the years, stated that a full context natural language is the best and most desirable human/system interface language. It is certainly true also that all systems designs are moving slowly toward this "highest" level language—in the United States—English. With the above situation in mind, a study group considered several possible scenarios:
>
> A. Continuation of the present state of affairs—the proliferation of more and more discrete command languages;
> B. Work toward agreement on the use of identical commands for identical functions;
> C. Create and provide an interface language link program inside and between each computer/communication system;
> D. Create and provide a full natural language (English) interface to be interposed between every user and each on-line retrieval system.

Each of the above scenarios were considered in terms of the following factors:

1. System considerations
2. Human factors
3. Timing required for creation and acceptance of change
4. Economic considerations.

Scenario A is the easiest from the viewpoint of individual system development. No coordination (and consequent system modification) would be imposed from sources external to each of the developing systems. From the user viewpoint, when two or more command languages must be learned, a saturation tolerance point is soon reached. Assuming a potential one million on-line STI system users, it was estimated that less than one half would ever routinely use even one format- ted command language. The other half would either use an information expert intermediary or not use the system at all. It was further estimated that less than one half of the user half would tolerate two formatted command languages; less than $\frac{1}{2}$ of that $\frac{1}{4}$ would tolerate three command languages, etc. These factors may be $\frac{1}{4}$ or $\frac{3}{4}$, but the point is that under this scenario, very few end users would be using the systems. Most access would be through intermediaries. The group concluded that there might be a slow consensus of common commands agreed to by the system operators over the years, but actions to date provide little optimism for this possibility. The overall economics of this scenario were deemed to be clearly unfavorable. The necessary training costs for hundreds of thousands of users would be staggering and it was concluded that most "trainees" would be "dropouts" (e.g., non-users) after little or no actual system use. The amounts of frustration and loss of efficiency would be (probably already is) hard to measure, but certainly is a significant factor.

Scenario B could be considered a subset of A and, in effect, is being tried at various levels right now. However, based on past experience, only modest success, at best, was visualized by the study group. When (if ever) we all agree to LOGON- LOGOFF or LOGIN-LOGOUT or whatever, I will be pleasantly encouraged to expect even greater "cooperation."

Scenario C had considerable attraction at first sight. It is relatively simple to accomplish in a system sense; it would require that each user be trained in only one command language, yet be able to use all the systems; it would be relatively simple to implement; it would be accepted by the users; and it would not be unreasonably expensive, either in initialization or continuing operation.

But all these expectations were based on the assumption that there would be economic incentives to the operating time sharing networks, and that there would only be two or three of them. Neither assumption proved to be true. Networks are proliferating broadly and rapidly and even assuming that the operators were willing to implement such software packages, the operational overhead would rise geometrically with the number of networks; e.g., 90 interlink programs would be required for 10 networks. A little further calculation easily persuaded us that this approach 1) was not economically feasible 2) was not likely to be implemented even if it were and 3) still required all users to be trained in one formatted com- mand language.

Scenario D appeared upon early consideration to be a difficult technical pro- blem; artificial intelligence seemed not too well developed; several major attempts had been made to develop free English input systems with no successful commercial development resulting therefrom. The technique appeared to be still in the experimental stages. From the user's viewpoint, however, it was agreed that this would be the best solution. Little or no training would be required, and the user base could broaden to its natural maximum. High system use would drive down unit search costs; the change would be minimal and easily accepted. No intermediaries would be required. If such a package could be developed, implementation would be relatively easy with minimal system perturbation. After a more careful review of this field, it was determined that artificial intelligence had, indeed, progressed sufficiently to provide a high probability of successfully producing a software package to provide a practical and useful full natural language interface that could be interposed between the on-line user and the Data Base Manager (DBM) of any typical medium to large scale computer of the type now being used by all the major data base vendors.

Based upon the information briefly summarized above, the study group concluded that, on balance, scenario D was the most attractive long term option considering the four factors described above. The new project resulting from this conclusion yielded ROBOT, a software preprocessor that translates English language requests into the command language of any high performance data base management system (DBMS), and translates the DBMS's response back into English for the user. The requests in the form of questions or commands, phrased in natural English, are automatically translated by ROBOT into the formal query language of the DBMS.

ROBOT is capable of providing an English language user interface for information retrieval and reporting from certain existing DBMS's. Sorting, basic computational functions, automatic columnar formatting, and a generalized interface to Data Processing routines are also provided. ROBOT has been interfaced with ADABAS, a powerful and very efficient DBMS. Interface work is underway for several other DBMS's. Utilizing the current state of the art in artificial intelligence and data base management, ROBOT is designed to allow continual extension of the artificial intelligence and DBMS capabilities, eg. pronoun reference has just been added.

It should be understood that ROBOT does not handle the totality of the syntactical variations of the English language, the totality of the possible DBMS functions or the totality of the great variety of data bases now available for querying on-line. What ROBOT does is to provide a system which can accommodate to reasonable and expected subsets of syntactic arrangements that are normally found in query type English sentences, and provide an interface to the most useful and expected DBMS functions related to a particular data base. Any new data base can be implemented with relative ease. Until very recently, the limits in all three of these above described parameters were so confining that no practical, full English command system was possible. It has been technically possible for some time to provide such systems, and perhaps even a much broader scope of natural language, DBMS functions, and data base varieties, but the limitation was primarily high cost.

The innovations embodied in ROBOT which make ROBOT the first such practical or commercially feasible system are: 1) use of the data base itself as the main dictionary or semantic store, so ROBOT's dictionary need contain primarily only linguistic terms; 2) drastic reduction in the size of the region in core memory required for the artificial intelligence functions; 3) drastic reduction in the CPU time required for analysis of each English request; 4) use of existing high performance DBMS's to manage the data; 5) preprocessor must be machine independent or "transportable" [pp. 223–226].[1]

The approach favored by Landau, the development of a natural language interface with the query languages of existing systems, also appears to be the one favored by Ackoff *et al.* (1976):

> Emphasis would be placed on providing users with easy-to-learn languages for preparation of their own procedures without having to work through a human intermediary—for example, by providing a retrieval language similar to the natural language combined with interactive aids from the computer to resolve ambiguities, diagnose errors, and assist the users in more precisely formulating their requests [p. 61].

The third approach mentioned by Landau, that of providing some type of switching language capable of converting automatically from one query language to another, has already been given considerable attention in some quarters. Work of this type has been conducted at the Electronic Systems Laboratory of MIT and reported by Reintjes and Marcus (1974) and Marcus and Reintjes (1977). Negus (1976) has undertaken a study to determine the feasibility of a standardized command set for EURONET. Although Landau refers to this approach as "relatively simple to accomplish in a system sense," it has proved not at all a simple problem.

Much work has also been done in the last 10 years on the possibility of achieving compatibility or convertibility among indexing vocabularies, as exemplified by the "intermediate lexicon" concept (see, for example, Horsnell, 1974) and by explorations of the feasibility of converting from one vocabulary to another automatically (Wall and Barnes, 1969). The importance of the multilingual problem is recognized in the existence of UNESCO guidelines on the construction of multilingual thesauri. Some work on automatic methods for the construction of interlingual thesauri is reported by Bollmann and Konrad (1976), and an approach to automatic indexing, with keyword translation, in a multilingual service has been described by Brisner (1975).

A system in which a user may converse with a data base containing text in English, German, French, and Swedish, and may use any one of these languages to interrogate the entire data base, is mentioned by Leimdörfer (1975). The most extensive multilingual system at the present time appears to be TITUS (Textile Information Treatment Users's

[1] This quotation is reproduced from Landau (1976) by permission of John Wiley & Sons, Inc.

Service), operated by the Institut Textile de France. In TITUS, automatic input and output translation is possible among the English, French, German, and Spanish languages.

The fourth problem mentioned earlier—that of enabling the on-line user to locate the most relevant file—seems to have received rather less attention. What is needed is some form of on-line referral data base that will tell an on-line user, for any preliminary inquiry he makes, which data bases have the greatest probability of satisfying his needs. In fact, the referral data base should have the capability of ranking substantive data bases according to the degree to which their characteristics match the characteristics of the preliminary inquiry. The on-line referral center would need to store, in one alphabetical sequence, the *vocabularies* of data bases accessible on-line. Any alphabetical vocabulary can be accommodated, whether in the form of thesaurus, list of subject headings, or list of keywords. In principle, the referral data base stores only the following data against each term:

1.   Identification of the data bases in which the term occurs
2.   The frequency with which the term occurs in each data base, where these figures are available

The on-line user, faced with a particular information need, calls up the referral center and puts in a preliminary inquiry. Depending on the type of matching algorithm adopted in implementation of the system, this inquiry may be some form of Boolean strategy, an unweighted list of terms, a weighted list of terms, or simply a description of the information need in sentence form. The inquiry is matched against the referral data base, and the substantive data bases referenced there are given a numerical score reflecting the probability that the data base will satisfy the information need. Presumably this score will reflect the degree of match between the terms of the inquiry and the terms of the data base, taking into account also the frequency with which various terms occur in various data bases. As output, which should be generated within seconds, the referral file will display a ranked list of data bases showing, against each, its numerical score in relation to the inquiry, and giving details as to how the file can be accessed (including, possibly, costs of interrogation).

A modest beginning toward such a referral data base is the issuance on microfiche, by Lockheed Information Systems, of vocabularies (DIALIST "merged indexes") consolidating the vocabularies of several data bases made available on-line by Lockheed. In 1976 the National Science Foundation awarded a grant to the Information Retrieval Research Laboratory, the University of Illinois, to undertake a feasibility study on an "automatic data base selector." This data base selector is very similar in concept to the referral data base mentioned above.

It seems likely that much more research will need to be undertaken in these critical intellectual areas and that, in the electronic information environment, we may see a resurgence of interest in the areas of automatic indexing, automatic abstracting, and even machine translation—areas of research that have been relatively dormant for almost a decade. Elsewhere, it has been pointed out (Lancaster, 1975) that the information systems of the future will need to be designed with the "end user" rather than the information specialist in mind. This will mean greater natural language orientation and the design of searching aids somewhat different from those we have at present. The field of linguistics (Lancaster, 1977) may have more to contribute to information science in the future than it has in the past.

There is some reason to suppose, too, that the information systems of the future will need to have capabilities beyond those of citation retrieval and document delivery. Data banks will provide highly structured files of scientific data for fact retrieval applications. Direct "question answering" from text, or at least the retrieval of answer-providing or answer-indicative passages of text (O'Connor, 1975), may also be expected by some users. Question-answering systems are considerably more difficult to design and implement on a large scale than document retrieval systems, and they require the use of more sophisticated techniques of linguistic analysis and representation.

Social and Psychological Problems

The social problems are likely to present the greatest obstacle to the achievement of an electronic information system in science. The electronic system represents a completely different way of "doing business." Conventional forms of publishing will disappear or, at least, assume greatly diminished significance. The conventional "unit" of scientific publishing, the scientific journal, if it does not disappear completely, will be recast into a very different form. Subscriptions, in a conventional sense, would be replaced by somewhat different methods of billing. There is also a copyright problem. This problem is difficult enough right now. It might be an order of magnitude more complex in a completely electronic system. The social problems, then, seem quite the most thorny. There will undoubtedly be great resistance to the whole idea of electronic communication in science, not so much from individual scientists, but from existing institutions, particularly the publishers of science materials. The respective roles of the primary publisher and of the secondary publisher must be completely redefined in the electronic world and, in fact, these roles may become much less clear than they are at present. The rather large initial capital investment in equipment might also be a discouragement to many publishers.

Some integration of primary and secondary publishing has already occurred (see Lerner 1974; Metzner, 1973) but this integration will be much more pronounced in the future. Lerner (1974) has recognized the tendency:

> The once clear-cut distinction between primary journal publishers and abstract-ing and indexing services is therefore becoming blurred, as we see secondary services composing full text for primary journals, and publishers offering abstracts on tape and in hard copy to secondary services [p. 115].

The functions of research libraries must also be redefined in the electronic environment. This matter is addressed in the next chapter.

Other social problems are related to the "publish or perish" phenomenon. It was pointed out by Herschman (1970) that the science journal exists to serve social and archival functions as well as the dissemination function. The first two of these functions it serves rather well. It is only in the dissemination activity that the journal really fails. The social function of the journal is related to the services it provides for authors. It gives them a suitable vehicle for communicating the results of their thought or research to the science community in a formal way. In the academic community at least, publication in respected professional journals is a necessary prerequisite to promotion, tenure, and other tan-gible rewards. There may not be any real problem in transferring the science reward system from print-on-paper to electronic publication, as long as the refereeing process is retained, but an author may get per-sonal gratification from seeing his work printed in a high-quality publica-tion, and this personal gratification might not extend to knowing that his work exists in some digital file, however prestigious this data base may be.

This leads us to a group of problems that are primarily psychological in origin. Will scientists be willing to adapt to a largely paperless environ-ment? The science community can be presumed to be both progressive and adaptable. There is every reason to suppose that the majority of scientists would be willing to adopt any system or device that can clearly be demonstrated to improve on the existing situation. The experience in the intelligence community suggests that even professionals who are initially hostile to the concept of paperless communication can be won over if the system benefits are clearly demonstrated. We also need to remember that we are conceptualizing, and will eventually be building, an electronic information system more for a future generation of scientists than for the present generation. To this new generation, on-line terminals are likely to be as commonplace as the telephone today, for almost certainly they will have used these devices routinely throughout the educational process.

It seems likely, however, that the on-line information systems of the future may need to be rather more user-oriented than most of those now in existence. This matter is raised by Ackoff *et al.* (1976):

> Although librarians and other information specialists will continue to play an important intermediate role in serving user needs, a strong emphasis would be placed on allowing direct user access to the System. This requires that the design of the SCATT System give considerable attention to human factors. The terminal equipment, languages used for inquiries, display of responses, and response times should be designed to recognize the needs of the user. Many users would be relatively unsophisticated and unfamiliar with the System; the System would provide them with on-line training and user aids. If at any point in the use of the System a person ran into difficulty—for example, not knowing what options were next available to him in formulating a complex inquiry—he would be able to ask the System for detailed guidance (e.g., a list of options, with perhaps an indication of the effectiveness and cost of each). The user experienced with the System could inhibit such detailed instructions, but would always be able to call for them when he encountered an unfamiliar situation. The System would also be able to detect automatically some user problems (e.g., too many erroneous responses) and provide assistance [p. 77].

The requirements for a more user-oriented on-line information system have also been enumerated by Lancaster (1971).

Finally, one must consider the possibility of certain medical problems being associated with prolonged use of video display devices. In a rather complete review of this subject, Östberg (1975) has identified a number of possible hazards, including various forms of muscular fatigue as well as extreme visual fatigue.

It is clear that many problems need to be solved before the electronic system can be fully implemented. Although some may be considered "thorny," none of them seem to present insuperable obstacles. If the majority of these problems are resolved, if systems can be made more user-oriented, and if benefits can be clearly demonstrated, the scientist of the year 2000 will not merely accept an electronic information system—he will demand it.

9

The Role of the Library
in a Paperless Society

In his discussion of a future electronic system, Folk (1977) suggests that "libraries would also wither away, their historic duty done [p. 79]." It now seems appropriate to consider this claim more closely. Will libraries be needed in an electronic information network? If so, what functions will they perform and how will they perform them?

The responsibilities and functions of the research library in an electronic world seem to have received rather little attention from the library profession at large. Indeed, projections by librarians on the future of the library are usually conservative in the extreme. Only Taylor (1975) has given a hint (and that a rather imprecise one) of what the future may hold:

> In the third scenario, the user becomes the center of the institution—not the systems, but the individuals in the community that is served. In this case the academic library will become a true switching center, a community center in which the dynamic process of negotiating and connecting users to people, materials, and media is the heart of the enterprise. This may happen both inside and outside the building called "a library." It will become a "library without walls" [p. 299].

It seems clear that librarians, and those who are responsible for the administration and funding of library services, must begin now to give serious consideration to what the library of the year 2000 may look like, assuming various levels of automation in the production and distribution of the primary and secondary literature of science. Possible interrelationships that might exist between the library and other institutions (e.g., primary and secondary publishers) in an electronic world must also be investigated. It will also be necessary to identify the actions (including appropriate changes in library education) that will be needed to move the profession from one dealing almost exclusively with print on paper to one dealing largely with electronic media.

What is needed, then, is a credible "transition scenario" for libraries, one spanning the period of the next 25 years. This chapter proposes to identify some of the more important questions that will need to be answered before such a scenario can be developed.

It seems that there are two main facets of the situation to be considered:

1. How will the library apply electronics to the handling of electronic materials?
2. How will the library apply electronics to the handling of printed, microform, and other materials, assuming that materials of this type still require processing, and how will the electronic processing of these materials be integrated with the electronic processing of the electronic materials?

The first question, of course, needs much more attention than the second, for the latter activities already occur in libraries in the form of automated acquisition, check-in, circulation, and similar procedures.

For each of the activities and services now performed by libraries, it will be necessary to consider whether the activity or service will (a) exist as at present; (b) exist in a different form; or (c) fail to exist at all. At the same time, activities and services that do not now exist, but might be feasible or required in an electronic environment, must be identified.

The possibility of primary and secondary publication and distribution in electronic form, coupled with the resulting ease of access to these data bases through on-line terminals, raises many important questions for libraries and librarians, including the following:

1. Will a library "own" a collection of electronic materials (i.e., data bases for which it has paid certain access rights) or will, essentially, all libraries have equal access to all materials on a pay-as-you-go basis?
2. If the latter, will there be any need for libraries at all? That is, will there be some people who need to access data bases and data

banks through libraries because they have no other access to the necessary terminals? Will libraries be able to offer services to users that they could not receive by going directly to data bases through their own terminals?

3. If libraries "own" electronic collections, how will these collections be selected and acquired? Will libraries still subscribe, for example, to an "applied physics" data base in electronic form in much the same way as they might now subscribe to the *Journal of Applied Physics?* Or will they be on the receiving end of some vast SDI service that automatically brings to their attention, or even adds to their collections, items that match their profiles of interest? Presumably, if electronic libraries actually do "own" electronic materials, both acquisition modes might exist, the former being perhaps more suitable for the academic library and the latter more suitable for the industrial or other highly specialized library.

4. If libraries do not own collections of materials, they presumably will have no responsibility for the bibliographic control of these materials. Which organizations, then, will assume the responsibility for cataloging and indexing operations?

5. If materials in digital form can all be accessed through on-line terminals, will there be any need for an electronic equivalent of interlibrary loan?

6. What are the implications of a paperless society for the education and training of librarians? What types of subject competence will be needed? What types of technical competence?

7. What are the implications for the organization and administration of research libraries?

At first sight, one might conclude that libraries and librarians will be completely redundant when the electronic system comes into existence. At least, one might conclude that they would exist only to preserve and provide services from the remnants of the printed literature. But, even in a society in which most potential users will have access to terminals capable of accessing data bases and data banks directly, it seems likely that some type of library service will still be needed.

For one thing, it seems reasonable to assume that some type of library will be needed to provide on-line access to resources for individuals who, for one reason or another, do not have their own terminals. The library will be a center in which access to data bases and data banks will be possible and in which trained personnel will be available to assist the user in the exploitation of these resources. The library may also serve as a "printout center." Even if a user has a terminal capable of interrogating a wide range of data bases, he may not have a high-speed printer available to him. The library may be the obvious source to which he turns to get a printout of items he needs to have in quantity in hard copy form.

Even in the electronic world, there will be a need for libraries to collect, catalog and index materials of purely local interest. Thus an industrial library will retain the responsibility of ensuring that the company's own literature—correspondence, technical reports, engineering drawings, contract files, and other forms—are indexed and accessible to potential users. Moreover, there may also exist libraries that index selected portions of the literature from a highly specialized point of view, a point of view not reflected in the publicly accessible data bases. A library in the rubber industry, for example, may survey an extremely wide range of scientific and technical literature in order to identify and specifically index all items of potential relevance to the population to be served. Thus items discussing interplanetary flight may be included in such a data base when they mention the application of rubber, even in a relatively minor way (e.g., as one component in the clothing of astronauts). Although such documents will be included in more general, publicly accessible files, they may not be indexed in these files under terms indicative of their relevance to the rubber industry.

If the great majority of the items with which libraries traditionally deal are available only in electronic form, however, what will be meant by the statement that a particular library "owns" a particular item (i.e., includes it in its collection), and how will a library select and acquire bibliographic items?

If we assume that some type of fee is charged by an electronic publisher for the right to access a particular data base, it is conceivable that libraries still will play a role in making materials accessible (free or at low cost) to a community of users. At the present time, a library may subscribe to a particular periodical at a cost identical to or somewhat above the cost to an individual subscriber. Yet the library's copy may be used by a great many scientists, whereas the individual subscription may be used by only one or two individuals. In the electronic world too, it is conceivable that a library might subscribe to the right to access a wide range of data bases and make these resources available to users, either free or at a cost appreciably less than that charged to individuals purchasing directly from publishers.

Assuming that libraries in some sense "collect" materials in the electronic world, what is involved in selection and collection? A library collects items in order to make them more accessible to the population the library is to serve, but in the electronic world, physical accessibility can hardly be improved by the interposition of a library between users and materials. Intellectual accessibility, however, can be improved. That is, through efficient selection procedures and appropriate, more specialized indexing techniques, a particular library could improve the accessibility of a segment of the literature most likely to be relevant to the interests of the users for whom the library is intended. In the electronic environment, then, a library might endeavor to select, from the universe of available resources, those items that have a high probability of being of interest to library users. The object of this selection is, through more precise indexing procedures, to make these items more intellectually accessible to the users of the library. Presumably, libraries can construct profiles of interest that can be matched at regular intervals against the characteristics of documents newly added to primary data bases.

One of the problems facing the future library is that of achieving some measure of integration between the processing of printed materials and the processing of electronic materials. Clearly, it is highly desirable that both types be handled as a single stream, rather than requiring entirely separate processing facilities. For many activities, integration can presumably be achieved rather easily. An on-line catalog, for example, can point equally effectively at resources in electronic, paper, or microimage form. The major difference between these materials is that those in paper form must be physically accessible in the library's own collections, while the microforms need not necessarily be (assuming the capability of transmitting video images from a remote store to user terminals), and most of the electronic resources "pointed to" by the catalog will presumably reside in central stores rather than in the library "collection" as such. Some library activities apply equally well to materials in electronic and paper form; for example, both are readily duplicated. Other activities apply to one but not the other. It is assumed that paper materials will continue to be borrowed from libraries, but it is less easy to visualize the need to "borrow" an electronic document. There will, of course, be a period of transition, in most libraries at least, during which some level of processing in parallel will be inevitable. The on-line catalog, for example, is likely to exist side by side with the card catalog for many years in the very large libraries since it may not prove cost-effective to undertake the conversion of millions of existing cards to machine-readable form.

It seems likely that librarians and other types of information specialists will still have important functions to perform in a paperless system. Presumably, people of this type would be needed for the indexing and abstracting of the primary literature. They would also be needed to construct indexing vocabularies and other tools required for the efficient exploitation of machine-readable resources. Although on-line terminals may be very widely available, and some type of on-line referral service may exist, it is probable that we will still need people to whom others can turn in the solution of particular information problems. There will still be a need for information specialists—people who are familiar with the resources available in machine-readable form and with the vocabularies, query languages, indexing techniques, and search strategies needed to exploit these resources most effectively. Even in the electronic world, there may still be individuals who prefer to delegate the task of information retrieval to others better qualified to undertake this task. Librarians in the electronic world may also have a more significant role to play in the training of scientists and others in the use of machine-readable resources. Training, in fact, could become a major activity of the librarian in the year 2000.

There is no reason to suppose that librarians need to continue to operate from "libraries." The closer we come to a completely electronic system, the less the need to conceive of libraries as physical entities bounded by walls. The "librarian" of the year 2000 may be a freelance information specialist, working from an office or from the home, to whom others turn for help in the exploitation of the rich variety of information resources available. In this environment, "consulting the librarian" would mean using a terminal to contact an information specialist.

The electronic age will force rather sweeping changes in the education and training of librarians. In a world in which many librarians will work from homes or offices, library science will no longer be defined in terms of "what goes on in a library." Indeed, this process of "de-institutionalization" of the librarian may, in the long run, prove very beneficial to his or her status and image in society. No other professional is as tied to an instituion as the librarian now is. The content of the curricula of library schools must change in order to place major emphasis on a knowledge of machine-readable resources and how to exploit these most effectively. For the effective exploitation of data bases, the librarian will need a rather thorough knowledge of indexing policies and procedures, the structure and characteristics of vocabularies used in data bases, query languages, searching strategies, and methods for optimizing interaction with potential customers. Probably, some knowledge of telecommunications technology will also be needed. These subjects are not now taught routinely in the majority of library schools, at least not to any degree of detail.

Although, as Folk (1977) suggests, libraries in the traditional sense may wither away in the electronic world, it seems rather improbable that the withering process will also affect librarians and other information specialists. Indeed, people of this background and experience may assume greatly increased importance in the future. Their libraries, however, may not be institutions with physical plants. Instead, they will consist of whatever resources the librarians have the wit to exploit from those available in the global information network. These libraries, as Taylor (1975) suggests, will truly be libraries without walls.

10

Conclusion

Although the science communication system of the future may not be identical in details with that suggested in this book, it is clear that we are moving rapidly and inexorably toward a system of this general type. The paperless system that is to come will be the culmination of a perfectly natural evolutionary process, the origins of which were traced in Chapter 2. The inevitability of these developments is one of simple economic necessity. The science communication system, as illustrated in Figure 5 (p. 53), cannot survive indefinitely in its present form. One who recognized this was Anderla (1973), who pointed out that, within 15 or 20 years, rising labor costs will make it impossible for any government to support the types of information processing activities that exist today. Computer processing offers the only possibility for coping with the situation because substantial improvements in manual productivity are infeasible. Anderla predicted that computer processing would be cheaper than manual processing for most information service activities by 1980.

All of the activities illustrated in Figure 5 are essential to science progress. Science research is sustained through assimilation of the results of previous investigation. This continuous assimilation depends on the accessibility of the literature of science through primary and secondary publication and through primary and secondary distribution. If the accessibility of the literature is reduced, assimilation is impeded and the progress of science is also curtailed.

While science as a whole continues in a period of expansion, the literature of science must continue to grow at a rapid rate. As discussed in Chapter 5, there is considerable evidence to suggest that conventional approaches to publication and distribution of science information will be unable to cope with a continued exponential growth of the literature. Two major choices exist: (a) to deliberately restrict the amount published and distributed, which would restrict the growth of science itself; or (b) to find alternative methods of packaging and disseminating the results of scientific investigation.

Even now one of the communication channels depicted in Figure 5—direct distribution of secondary publications to the science community—is virtually nonexistent since most of the major secondary publications are already too expensive for the individual subscriber. The costs of secondary publication would continue to escalate even if these services maintained present publishing levels, without any attempt to keep up with growth in the primary literature. When ever-increasing production costs are compounded by the need to grow with the literature, it is inevitable that substantial price increases will continue as long as these secondary services remain in printed form. What must an annual subscription to *Chemical Abstracts* cost when the service is covering a million items each year? The results of these trends are quite obvious. Secondary publications, already almost exclusively to be found in institutions, will price themselves beyond the resources of the small institutions and will be found only in the larger, wealthier organizations. The same fate, although substantially delayed, will attend primary publication in conventional form. The printed science journal in conventional form is likely to price itself beyond the resources of the individual scientist so that, eventually, science journals will be found only in libraries. Other "conceptual alternatives" to the science journal, as discussed by Lancaster and Brown (1969), might delay this process, but only a move to electronic production and dissemination can reverse it.

Through conventional methods of information handling, then, the science literature can only become progressively less accessible to the science community as a whole, at least while science continues in a period of exponential growth. However, as we have seen through this book, increasing automation tends to improve the accessibility of the literature. It is quite clear, in fact, that manual processing will become increasingly costly and will continue to affect accessibility adversely, while computer processing will become increasingly economical in comparison and will continue to improve the accessibility of the literature.

We are already very close to the day in which a great science library could exist in a space less than 10 feet square. Right now a single on-line terminal can give a small organization, or even a single individual, access to perhaps 50 different data bases. Within a short time, several hundred will be accessible on-line. On a pay-as-you-go, on-line access basis, vast resources can be made economically available to organizations and individuals that could in no way afford to subscribe to the equivalent printed services. At current prices, it could cost a six-figure sum annually for the privilege of having on the shelves of a library a fairly comprehensive collection of secondary publications in science. It must also be recognized that the on-line access provides search capabilities that are a great improvement over the search capabilities of the printed tool. Moreover, some specialized data bases, or data banks, exist only in machine-readable form. They are accessible in the electronic world but not in the world of paper. It is true that not all indexing and abstracting services are now accessible on-line, but a great many already are and the number is steadily rising. It seems entirely reasonable to suppose that a small industrial research library, within a few years, might consist largely of a few terminals potentially connectable to several hundred data bases and data banks of a scientific or technical nature. Access to equivalent resources in printed form would be quite out of the question.

As mentioned earlier, the computer has been applied at a substantial level only to certain of the information transfer activities illustrated in Figure 5. So far, the computer has been applied most extensively in steps 1, 7, and 9, less extensively in steps 5, 6, and 8, and almost not at all in steps 2, 3, 4, and 10. In the long run, however, the continued existence of this communication cycle will require the application of computers to all stages. We are at present in an interim phase in the automation of science communication. This interim phase is one in which machine-readable data bases exist side by side with printed data bases. The computer is used to produce a conventional printed publication which is also distributed conventionally. But this must change. As depicted in Figure 16, our present stage of development is one that represents great advances in the electronic production of secondary publications in printed form, with a growth from one to several hundred such data bases in about a decade. At some date in the near future, there will begin a natural crossover from electronic production of print to electronic publication and dissemination (i.e., to the paperless mode of operation). The same evolutionary process will apply to the production of primary publications, but the evolution in primary publication will lag some years behind the development in secondary publication. By the year 2000, it seems entirely reasonable to suppose that formal com-

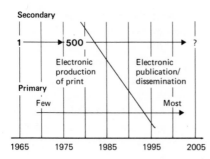

Figure 16. Evolution from print on paper to electronic publication of science information.

munication in science and technology will be almost exclusively electronic, and that a substantial move to machine-aided informal communication will also have occurred. Such changes seem to be simply a matter of economic necessity, a. fact that was clearly recognized in a report from PA International Management Consultants (1974):

> Cost trends in both publishing and computer searching of scientific and technical information are unambiguous. Electronic distribution of STI will inevitably replace printed distribution. Connections will be established between STI networks and publishers, and many journals will come to exist only in electronic form [p. 71].

These developments seem as inevitable in the social sciences as they are in the sciences, although the adoption of paperless communication in some branches of the social sciences may lag several years behind its adoption in the sciences.

What are the steps that can be expected to occur in the transition from the system as it is today to a completely electronic system? It is difficult to be definite about this, but it seems likely that the major impetus will come from the consumers of information rather than the producers. There is likely to be considerable inertia in much of the publishing industry. Indeed, the present concern of publishers of science journals seems to be that of "saving" the journal in more or less its present form. Many alternatives to the present journal format have been suggested and several of these have already been implemented. Such alternatives, involving the use of paper or microforms or both, can only be considered as stopgap measures. The real problem to be addressed is not "How can we save the existing system?" but "How can we design a new system, with greater efficiency and additional capabilities, that will much better meet the needs of the information consumer?"

Probably, the first electronic journals will actually be new journals, produced by new publishers (e.g., groups of users working in a computer conferencing environment), rather than electronic replacements for existing titles. The conversion of existing journals to electronic form will occur somewhat later, as a gradual process, when the necessary telecommunications structure and a receptive market have been shown to exist. Roistacher (1978) agrees that the user community is likely to provide the necessary pressure:

> Virtual journals will be founded in communities of scholars who have access to computer networks and who believe in virtual journals. The crucial social aspect of a virtual journal is not merely that scholars submit articles but that they read and cite articles in virtual journals at least as frequently as conventionally published work [p. 6].

Woodward (1976) also suggests that new journals will be the first to emerge in the electronic environment:

> Whilst it is acknowledged that the technology is currently feasible and that the economics will be favourable within a few years, the traditions of paper publishing, the problems of adaptation by authors, publishers, libraries and users, and the totally different patterns of investment required indicate that the introduction of electronic media for dissemination of scientific information will be both slow and piecemeal. Successful introduction of electronic journals will probably be in new subject areas not already served by conventional media, and will provide a communication system that is less formal than that which currently exists [p. 1].

The developments in primary publishing are likely to follow closely the developments that have already taken place in secondary publishing. We should see a period in which primary text will be available in both printed and machine-readable form. The machine-readable text will be accessible through some type of on-line retailer in much the same way that the secondary data bases are at present. Perhaps the same retailers will handle both primary and secondary publications. Folk (1977) suggests that the network structure already exists and that it is now a very short step to the paperless system:

> A distributed SIS is emerging without any plan or central direction. Not only is DIALOG available on Telenet, but several universities (such as MIT) have computers on the network. Thus, the indexing system and user hosts already are interconnected. All that is necessary for SIS to exist is that one or more publishers place their machine-readable texts on a network computer. An organization such as the American Chemical Society or the Institute of Electrical and Electronic Engineers could make part or all of their future publications available in this manner. Indexes could indicate the articles that were available and the host address. As journal hosts joined the network, a computerized scientific information system would emerge [p. 78].

Before the paperless system can be implemented on a large scale, however, a rather substantial change in the market for information services must occur. The change needed is a reversal of the present balance between consumers of printed services and consumers of electronic services. At the present time, most of the cost of creating a machine-readable data base is borne by the subscribers to the printed version. The users of the electronic version are partly subsidized by these subscribers since the volume of use of the machine-readable file, and the resulting income from royalties, leasing arrangements, and licensing agreements, is as yet far from sufficient to support the costs of creating the data base. This situation will change and we can expect to see the market for electronic services growing at a very rapid pace while, at the same time, the market for the printed services will steadily decline. To take an obvious example, it seems highly unlikely that a great untapped market exists for *Chemical Abstracts* in printed form. It is certain, however, that a large potential market still exists for on-line access to this data base on a pay-as-you-go basis. The demand for electronic access to this and other secondary data bases, then, can be expected to increase very substantially over the next decade, while the demand for the printed analogs will decline. It is only a matter of time before the size of the "electronic user" market, when coupled with realistic pricing strategies, is adequate to support the costs of building and maintaining the data base. At this point, the electronic version becomes the main product. Thereafter, we can expect the rather rapid demise of the printed version. Clearly, these developments will first take place with secondary publications. The same sequence of events will occur with the science journal, although the developments will occur some years later.

The paperless society is rapidly approaching, whether we like it or not. Everyone reading this book will be affected by it in one way or another. We cannot bury our heads in the sand. We may choose to ignore the electronic world, but this will not make it go away. Now is the time for responsible organizations to study the implications of the rapid technological changes that are occurring for the operations of publishers, primary and secondary, for the operations of libraries and information centers, and for the individual scientist as producer and user of information. If we do not plan now for the years ahead, we may find the transition to be one of disruption and chaos rather than one of ordered evolutionary progress.

References

Ackoff, R. L. *et al.* (1976). *Designing a National Scientific and Technological Communication System.* Philadelphia: University of Pennsylvania Press.

Allen, T. J. (1966). *Managing the Flow of Scientific and Technological Information.* Cambridge, Mass.: Alfred P. Sloan School of Management, MIT.

Allen, T. J. (1975). "The Importance of Direct Personal Communication in the Transfer of Technology." In North Atlantic Treaty Organization, Advisory Group for Aerospace Research and Development, *The Problem of Optimization of User Benefit in Scientific and Technological Information Transfer,* 2-1–2-10. Paris. AGARD-CP-179.

Allen, T. J., and P. G. Gerstberger (1967). *Criteria for Selection of an Information Source.* Cambridge, Mass.: Alfred P. Sloan School of Management, MIT.

Allen, T. J., J. M. Piepmeier, and S. Cooney (1971). "The International Technological Gatekeeper." *Technology Review,* 73, 37–43.

American Psychological Association (1963). *Reports of the American Psychological Association's Project on Scientific Information Exchange in Psychology,* Vol. 1, Washington, D.C.

Anderla, G. (1973). *Information in 1985: A Forecasting Study of Information Needs and Resources.* Paris: Organisation for Economic Cooperation and Development.

Arthur D. Little, Inc. (1974). *A Survey of Technologies Applicable to Electronic Mail Handling Systems.* Report to the United States Postal Service. PB-252 821.

Ashmole, R. F., D. E. Smith, and B. T. Stern (1973). "Cost-Effectiveness of Current Awareness Services in the Pharmaceutical Industry." *Journal of the American Society for Information Science,* 24, 29–39.

Ashworth, W. (1974). "The Information Explosion." *Library Association Record,* 76, 63–68, 71.

Bagdikian, B. H. (1971). *The Information Machines: Their Impact on Men and the Media.* New York: Harper & Row.

Bamford, H., Jr. (1973). "The Editorial Processing Center." *IEEE Transactions on Professional Communication,* PC-16, 82–83.

Bar-Hillel, Y. (1963). "Is Information Retrieval Approaching a Crisis?" *American Documentation,* 14, 95–98.

Barr, K. P. (1967). "Estimates of the Number of Currently Available Scientific and Technical Periodicals." *Journal of Documentation,* 23, 110–116.

Baumol, W. J., and M. Marcus (1973). *Economics of Academic Libraries.* Washington, D.C.: American Council on Education.

Baumol, W. J., and J. A. Ordover (1976). "Public Good Properties in Reality: The Case of Scientific Journals." Paper presented at the Annual Conference of the American Society for Information Science, San Francisco. (Available on microfiche as part of the proceedings of the ASIS Annual Meeting, 1976.)

Bell, D. (1977) "Teletext and Technology." *Encounter,* 48, 9–29.

Bernal, J. D. (1959). "The Transmission of Scientific Information. A User's Analysis." *International Conference on Scientific Information,* Washington, D.C., November 16–21, 1958, 2 vols. Washington, D.C.: National Academy of Sciences, National Research Council, 77–95.

Bertram, S. J. K. (1970). "The Relationship between Intra-Document Citation Location and Citation Level." Unpublished Ph.D. dissertation, University of Illinois, Graduate School of Library Science.

Bitzer, D. L., and D. Skaperdas (1972). *The Design of an Economically Viable Large-Scale Computer-Based Education System.* Urbana, Ill.: University of Illinois, Computer-based Education Research Laboratory.

Bollmann, P., and E. Konrad (1976). "Automatic Association Methods in the Construction of Interlingual Thesauri." Paper presented at EURIM 2, European Conference on the Application of Research in Information Services and Libraries, Amsterdam, March 23–25, 1976.

Borman, L., and B. Mittman (1972). "Interactive Search of Bibliographic Data Bases in an Academic Environment." *Journal of the American Society for Information Science,* 23, 164–171.

Bradford, S. C. (1948). *Documentation.* London: Crosby Lockwood.

Brisner, O. (1975). "Test Results on Automatic Indexing and Keyword Translation for a Multilingual Documentation Service." Paper presented at the Fifth Cranfield International Conference on Mechanized Information Storage and Retrieval Systems, Cranfield, England, July 22–25, 1975.

Brookes, B. C. (1973). "Numerical Methods of Bibliographic Analysis." *Library Trends,* 22, 18–43.

Brown, W. S., J. R. Pierce, and J. F. Traub (1967). "The Future of Scientific Journals." *Science,* 158, 1153–1159.

Buckland, M. K. (1972). "Are Obsolescence and Scattering Related?" *Journal of Documentation,* 28, 242–245.

Burchinal, L. G. (1975). "Microforms and Electronic Publication: Emerging Bases for Scientific Communication." *IEEE Transactions on Professional Communication.* PC-18, 3, 174–176.

Burton, H. D., and T. B. Yerke (1969). "Famulus, a Computer-Based System for Augmenting Personal Documentation Efforts." *Proceedings of the American Society for Information Science,* 6, 53–56.

Bush, V. (1945). "As We May Think." *Atlantic Monthly,* 176, 101–108.

Carlson, J. A. (1973). "Video Editing." In *Technological Change in Printing and Publishing*, ed. L. H. Hattery and G. P. Bush. New York: Spartan Books, distributed by Hayden Books, Rochelle Park, N.J., 105–124.

Clayton, A., and N. Nisenoff (1976). *A Forecast of Technology for the Scientific and Technical Information Communities*, 4 vols. Arlington, Va.: Forecasting International Inc. PB-253 937.

Coleman, J., E. Katz, and H. Menzel (1966). *Medical Innovation: A Diffusion Study*. Indianapolis: Bobbs-Merrill.

Cooper, M. (1968). "Current Information Dissemination: Ideas and Practices." *Journal of Chemical Documentation*, 8, 207–218.

Crane, D. (1972). *Invisible Colleges: Diffusion of Knowledge in Scientific Communities*. Chicago: University of Chicago Press.

Crawford, S. (1971). "Informal Communications among Scientists in Sleep Research." *Journal of the American Society for Information Science*, 22, 301–310.

Cummings, M. M. (1967). "Needs in the Health Sciences." In *Electronic Handling of Information: Testing and Evaluation*, ed. A. Kent *et al.* Washington, D.C.: Thompson, 13–23.

Day, L. H. (1973). "An Assessment of Travel/Communications Substitutability." *Futures*, 5,6, 559–572.

De Gennaro, R. (1977). "Escalating Journal Prices: Time to Fight Back." *American Libraries*, 8, 2, 69–74.

DeGrolier, E. (1975). "On the Use of Quantitative Data in Information Science." In North Atlantic Treaty Organization, Advisory Group for Aerospace Research and Development, *The Problem of Optimization of User Benefit in Scientific and Technological Information Transfer*, 7-1–7-9. Paris. AGARD-CP-179.

Dunn, O. C., D. L. Tolliver, and R. S. Tolliver (1972). *The Past and Likely Future of 58 Research Libraries, 1951–1980: A Statistical Study of Growth and Change.* 1970–1971. Layfayette, Ind.: Purdue University Libraries.

Egan, M., and H. H. Henkle (1956). "Ways and Means in Which Research Workers, Executives, and Others Use Information." In *Documentation in Action*, ed. J. H. Shera *et al.* New York: Reinhold, 137–159.

Elsdon-Dew, R. (1955). "The Library from the Point of View of the Research Worker." *South African Libraries*, 23, 51–54.

Folk, H. (1977). "The Impact of Computers on Book and Journal Publication." In *The Economics of Library Automation: Proceedings of the 1976 Clinic on Library Applications of Data Processing*, ed. J. L. Divilbiss. Urbana, Ill.: University of Illinois, Graduate School of Library Science, 72–82.

Fry, B. M., and H. S. White (1975). *Economics and Interaction of the Publisher–Library Relationship in the Production and Use of Scholarly and Research Journals.* Bloomington, Ind.: Indiana University, Graduate Library School. PB-249 108. Also published as *Publishers and Libraries: A Study of Scholarly and Research Journals.* Lexington, Mass.: Lexington Books, 1976.

Garvey, W. D., and B. C. Griffith (1964). *The Discovery and Dissemination of Scientific Information among Psychologists in Two Research Environments.* Washington, D.C.: American Psychological Association. PB-166 414.

Garvey, W. D., and B. C. Griffith (1972). "Communication and Information Processing within Scientific Disciplines: Empirical Findings for Psychology." *Information Storage and Retrieval*, 8, 123–136.

Garvey, W. D., N. Lin, and C. E. Nelson (1970). "Communication in the Physical and the Social Sciences." *Science*, 170, 1166–1173.

Glantz, R. S. (1970). "SHOEBOX—A Personal File Handling System for Textual Data." *AFIPS Conference Proceedings, Fall Joint Computer Conference*, 37, 535–545.

Green, D. (1967). "Death of an Experiment." *International Science and Technology*, May, 82–88.

Hamburger, J. (1973). "Le Rejet des Greffes." *La Recherche*, 36, 671–675.

Heaps, H. S. (1975). "Data Compression of Large Document Data Bases." *Journal of Chemical Information and Computer Sciences*, 15, 32–39.

Heenan, W. F., and D. C. Weeks (1971). *Informal Communication Among Scientists*. Washington, D.C.: George Washington University, Biological Sciences Communication Project.

Herschman, A. (1970). "The Primary Journal: Past, Present, and Future." *Journal of Chemical Documentation*, 10, 37–42.

Hertz, D. B., and A. H. Rubenstein (1954). *Team Research*. New York: Columbia University, Department of Industrial Engineering.

Hillman, D. J. (1973). "Customized User Services Via Interactions with LEADERMART." *Information Storage and Retrieval*, 9, 587–596.

Horsnell, V. (1974). *Intermediate Lexicon for Information Science: A Feasibility Study*. London: Polytechnic of North London, School of Librarianship.

Johns Hopkins University. Center for Research in Scientific Communication (1970). *The Role of the National Meeting in Scientific and Technical Communication*. Baltimore, Md., 455pp.

Kemeny, J. G. (1972). *Man and the Computer*. New York: Scribner.

Kilgour, F. G., P. L. Long, A. L. Landgraf, and J. A. Wyckoff (1972). "The Shared Cataloging System of the Ohio College Library Center." *Journal of Library Automation*, 5, 157–183.

King, D. W., *et al.* (1976). *Statistical Indicators of Scientific and Technical Communication (1960–1980)*, Vol. 2. Rockville, Md.: King Research Inc., Center for Quantitative Sciences.

Kuney, J. H. (1973). "Primary Journals." In *Technological Change in Printing and Publishing*, ed. L. H. Hattery and G. P. Bush. New York: Spartan Books, distributed by Hayden Books, Rochelle Park, N.J., 125–133.

Lancaster, F. W. (1971). "Are We Ready for On-Line Information Retrieval?" *Proceedings of the 1971 Annual Conference of the Association for Computing Machinery*, 565–568.

Lancaster, F. W. (1972). *Vocabulary Control for Information Retrieval*. Washington, D.C.: Information Resources Press.

Lancaster, F. W. (1974). "A Study of Current Awareness Publications in the Neurosciences." *Journal of Documentation*, 30, 255–272.

Lancaster, F. W. (1975). "Vocabulary Control for On-Line, Interactive Retrieval Systems: Requirements and Possible Approaches." Paper presented at the Third International Study Conference on Classification Research, Bombay, January 6–11, 1975.

Lancaster, F. W. (1977). "Perspective Paper: Information Science." In *Natural Language in Information Science*, ed. D. E. Walker *et al.* Stockholm: Skriptor, 19–43.

Lancaster, F. W., and A. M. Brown (1969). *Conceptual Alternatives to the Scientific Journal*. Bethesda, Md.: Westat Research Inc.

Lancaster, F. W., and E. G. Fayen (1973). *Information Retrieval On-Line*. Los Angeles: Melville (Wiley).

Landau, R. M. (1976) "ROBOT: an English Language Query Facility for Use With Data Base Management and Retrieval Systems." *Proceedings of the ASIS Annual Meet-*

ing, vol. 13, 1976, p. 43 (abstract). (The full paper appears as pp. 222–232 of the microfiche released with the abstracts of the meeting.)

Landau, R. M. (1977). *ROBOT: the Highest Level Human/Machine Interface Language Processor for Online Interactive Information Retrieval*. Kensington, Md.: Science Information Association.

Leimdörfer, M. (1975). "Information Retrieval and the Mini-Computer." In *The Interactive Library: Computerized Processes in Library and Information Networks*, ed. S. Schwarz. Proceedings of a seminar held in Stockholm, November 25–28, 1974. Stockholm: Swedish Society for Technical Documentation, 227–239.

Leimkuhler, F. F., and A. E. Neville (1968). "The Uncertain Future of the Library." *Wilson Library Bulletin*, 43, 30–38.

Leith, J. D. (1969). "Biomedical Literature: An Analysis of Journal Articles Collected by a Radiation-and-Cell-Biologist." *American Documentation*, 20, 143–148.

Lerner, R. G. (1974). "The Use of the Computer in Converting Primary Information." *Journal of Chemical Documentation*, 14, 112–115.

Licklider, J. C. R. (1965). *Libraries of the Future*. Cambridge, Mass.: MIT Press.

Lin, N., W. D. Garvey, and C. E. Nelson (1970). "A Study of the Communication Structure of Science." In *Communication among Scientists and Engineers*, ed. C. E. Nelson and D. K. Pollock. Lexington, Mass.: D.C. Heath, 23–60.

Marcus, R. S., and J. F. Reintjes (1977). *Computer Interfaces for User Access to Heterogeneous Information Retrieval Systems*. Cambridge, Mass.: MIT, Electronic Systems Laboratory. ESL-R-739.

Martin, J., and A. R. D. Norman (1970). *The Computerized Society*. Englewood Cliffs, N.J.: Prentice-Hall.

Martyn, J. (1964). "Unintentional Duplication of Research." *New Scientist*, 377, 338.

McHale, J. (1972). "The Changing Information Environment: A Selective Topography." In *Information Technology: Some Critical Implications for Decision Makers*. New York: The Conference Board, 183–238.

Mellanby, K. (1967). "A Damp Squib." *New Scientist*, March 23, 626–627.

Metzner, A. W. K. (1973). "Integrating Primary and Secondary Journals: A Model for the Immediate Future." *IEEE Transactions on Professional Communication*, PC-16, 84–91, 175–176.

Mittman, B., and W. D. Dominick (1973). "Developing Monitoring Techniques for an On-Line Information Retrieval System." *Information Storage and Retrieval*, 6, 297–307.

Moghdam, D. (1978). *Computers in Newspaper Publishing*. New York: Marcel Dekker, Inc.

Mooers, C. N. (1960). "Mooers' Law or, Why Some Retrieval Systems Are Used and Others Are Not." *American Documentation*, 11, No. 3, ii.

Moore, J. A. (1972). "An Inquiry on New Forms of Primary Publications." *Journal of Chemical Documentation*, 12, 75–78.

Narin, F., and M. P. Carpenter (1974). *National Publication and Citation Comparisons*. Cherry Hill, N.J.: Computer Horizons Inc.

National Academy of Sciences–National Academy of Engineering (1970). *Report of the Task Group on the Economics of Primary Publication*. Washington, D.C.

National Science Foundation (1964). *Characteristics of Scientific Journals 1949–1959*. Washington, D.C.

National Science Foundation (1975). Request for Proposal 75-136, A Systems Analysis of Scientific and Technical Communication in the United States. Washington, D.C., National Science Foundation, August 14, 1975.

Needham, R. M. (1961). *Research on Information Retrieval, Classification and Grouping, 1957–61.* Cambridge, England: Cambridge Language Research Unit. Report No. ML 149.

Negus, A. E. (1976). *Study to Determine the Feasibility of a Standardized Command Set for EURONET.* London: The Institution of Electrical Engineers.

O'Connor, J. (1975). "Retrieval of Answer-Sentences and Answer-Figures from Papers by Text Searching." *Information Processing and Management,* 11, 155–164.

Organisation for Economic Cooperation and Development (1971). *Information for a Changing Society.* Paris.·

Östberg, O. (1975). "CRTs Pose Health Problems for Operators." *International Journal of Occupational Health and Safety,* 44, 6, 24–26, 50, 52.

PA International Management Consultants, Ltd. (1974). *Forecast of Users of On-Line Retrieval Services for Scientific and Technical Information in Europe 1976–1985.* Paris: Commission of the European Communities.

Parker, E. B. (1975). "Social Implications of Computer/Telecommunications Systems." Paper presented at the OECD Conference on Computer/Telecommunications Policy, Paris, February 4–6, 1975.

Pratt, G. (1975). *Data Bases in Europe.* London: ASLIB.

Price, C. R. (1975). "Conferencing via Computer: Cost Effective Communication for the Era of Forced Choice." In H. A. Linstone, and M. Turoff, *The Delphi Method: Techniques and Applications,* Reading, Mass.: Addison-Wesley, 497–516.

Price, D. J. de Solla (1963). *Little Science, Big Science.* New York: Columbia University Press.

Price, D. J. de Solla (1964). "Ethics of Scientific Publication." *Science,* 144, 655–657.

Price, D. J. de Solla (1974). Remarks on the report *Information in 1985* by G. Anderla, *Information,* Part 2, 3, No. 3, 32–37.

Rees, A. M., *et al.* (1967). *A Field Experimental Approach to the Study of Relevance Assessments in Relation to Document Searching.* Cleveland: Case Western Reserve University, Center for Documentation and Communication Research.

Reintjes, J. F., and R. S. Marcus (1974). *Research in the Coupling of Interactive Information Systems.* Final Report. Cambridge, Mass.: MIT, Electronic Systems Laboratory. ESL-FR-556.

Reitman, W., *et al.* (1969). "AUTONOTE: A Personal Information Storage and Retrieval System." *Proceedings of the 24th National Conference of the Association for Computing Machinery,* 67–76.

Roistacher, R. C. (1978). "The Virtual Journal," *Computer Networks,* 2, 18–24.

Rosenberg, V. (1966). *The Application of Psychometric Techniques to Determine the Attitudes of Individuals Toward Information Seeking.* Bethlehem, Pa.: Lehigh University, Center for the Information Sciences.

Rule, D. F. (1975). "Character Sets." *Journal of Chemical Information and Computer Sciences,* 15, 31–32.

Sackman, H., and N. Nie, eds. (1970). *The Information Utility and Social Choice.* Montvale, N.J.: AFIPS Press.

Salisbury, B. A., Jr. and H. E. Stiles (1969). "The Use of the B-Coefficient in Information Retrieval." *Proceedings of the American Society for Information Science,* 6, 265–268.

Salton, G. (1968). *Automatic Information Organization and Retrieval.* New York: McGraw-Hill.

Salton, G. (1975). *Dynamic Information and Library Processing.* Englewood Cliffs, N.J.: Prentice-Hall.

Sandoval, A. M., A Büttenklepper, M. Villamechel, and J. Ruiz-Gusils. (1976)." The Vehicles of the Results of Latin American Research: A Bibliometric Approach." Paper presented at the 38th World Congress of FID, Mexico City, September 27–October 1, 1976.

Senders, J. W. *et al.* (1975). *Scientific Publications Systems: An Analysis of Past, Present and Future Methods of Scientific Communication.* Toronto: Toronto University. PB-242 259.

Senders, J. W. (1976). "The Scientific Journal of the Future." *American Sociologist,* 11, 160–164.

Senders, J. W. (1977). "An On-Line Scientific Journal." *The Information Scientist,* 11, 1, 3–9.

Shephard, D. A. E. (1973). "Some Effects of Delay in Publication of Information in Medical Journals, and Implications for the Future." *IEEE Transactions on Professional Communication,* PC-16, 3, 143–147, 181.

Sondak, N. E., and R. J. Schwarz (1973). "The Paperless Journal." *Chemical Engineering Progress,* 69, 1, 82–83.

Soper, M. E. (1972). "The Relationship Between Personal Collections and the Selection of Cited References." Unpublished Ph.D. dissertation, University of Illinois, Graduate School of Library Science.

Sorokin, U. N. (1968). "A Possible Perspective for the Primary and Secondary Scientific Publications." Paper presented at the I.C.S.U. Abstracting Board General Assembly, Goslar, Germany, July, 1968.

Sparck Jones, K. (1971). *Automatic Keyword Classification for Information Retrieval.* Hamden, Conn.: Archon Books.

Sparck Jones, K. (1974). *Automatic Indexing 1974: A State of the Art Review.* Cambridge, University of Cambridge, Computer Laboratory.

Stetten, K. J. (1971a). *Interactive Television Software for Cable Television Application.* Washington, D.C.: Mitre Corporation. MTP-354.

Stetten, K. J. (1971b). *TICCIT: A Delivery System Designed for Mass Utilization.* Washington, D.C.: Mitre Corporation. M71-56.

Stevens, M. E. (1970). *Automatic Indexing: A State-of-the-Art Report.* Washington, D.C.: National Bureau of Standards. NBS Monograph 91.

Stifle, J. (1971). *A Plasma Display Terminal.* Urbana, Ill.: University of Illinois, Computer-based Education Research Laboratory.

Stiles, H. E. (1961). "Machine Retrieval Using the Association Factor." *Machine Indexing: Progress and Problems.* Washington, D.C.: American University School of Government and Public Administration, 192–206.

Taylor, R. S. (1975). "Patterns Toward a User-Centered Academic Library." In *New Dimensions for Academic Library Service,* ed. E. J. Josey, Metuchen, N.J.: The Scarecrow Press, 298–304.

Thompson, G. B. (1976). "Towards a Clever Data Network." *Computer Networks,* 1, 2, 111–118.

Turoff, M. (1973). "Conferencing via Computer." *Information Networks Conference,* NEREM, 1973, 194–197.

Van Dam, A., and D. C. Rice (1971). "On-Line Text Editing: A Survey," *Computing Surveys,* 3, 93–114.

Volk, J. (1971). *The Reston, Virginia, Test of the Mitre Corporation's Interactive Television System.* Washington, D.C.: Mitre Corporation. MTP-352.

Wall, E., and J. Barnes (1969). *Intersystem Compatibility and Convertibility of Subject Vocabularies.* Philadelphia: Auerbach Corporation. PB-184 144.

Wallace, E. M. (1966). "User Requirements, Personal Indexes, and Computer Support." *Proceedings of the American Documentation Institute*, 3, 73–80.

White, M. D. (1971). "Communications Behavior of Academic Economists." Unpublished Ph.D. dissertation, University of Illinois, Graduate School of Library Science. (Available from University Microfilms.)

Williams, J. H., Jr. (1969). *BROWSER: An Automatic Indexing On-Line Text Retrieval System*. Annual progress report. Gaithersburg, Md.: IBM Federal Systems Division. AD-693 143.

Williams, M. E., and W. T. Brandhorst (1976). "Data About Data Bases." *Bulletin of the American Society for Information Science*, 3, 2, 20–21.

Woodward, A. M. (1976). *The Electronic Journal—An Assessment*. London: ASLIB. British Library R & D Report No. 5322.

Yasaki, E. K. (1975). "Toward the Automated Office." *Datamation*, Vol. 21, No. 2, 59–62.

Yokote, G., and R. A. Utterback (1974). "Time Lapses in Information Dissemination: Research Laboratory to Physician's Office." *Bulletin of the Medical Library Association*, 62, 251–257.

Zipf, G. K. (1949). *Human Behavior and the Principle of Least Effort*. Cambridge, Mass.: Addison-Wesley.

Index